PRAISE FOR
Stories: Finding Your Wings

Stories: Finding Your Wings *delivers an entertaining account and perspective on the life of Heidi Allen and offers the perfect example of how shedding the layers and looking deep within can transform your life. Her truthful yet simple way of storytelling is not only compelling for readers —but it drives home the point that anything is possible when we choose to be positive—letting go of negativity. The book is an excellent tool for anyone wanting to make a change in their life and a difference in the lives of others. I found Heidi's honesty refreshing, powerful, and relatable in this book—especially when it comes to navigating our own lives. Whether it was sending that fateful text, having a meltdown in Costco or the blog idea that grew into an online movement—readers will find Heidi's personal stories identifiable—and that's the charming reality behind this book.* Finding Your Wings *is a fast, enjoyable read that will leave you thinking about the proverbial phrase "Is the glass half empty or half full?" Each story provides teachable moments for those who dare to take risks despite their fears to find happiness.*
- Susan Hay, Broadcast Journalist, Global News, Toronto

Like the traveller in the Paulo Coelho's book The Alchemist, *in* Stories: Finding Your Wings, *Heidi is on a brave, adventure-filled expedition fraught with "right place at the right time" moments that encapsulate her life! We get to witness her drive to live authentically, sometimes causing her great strife, yet heroically managing to repeatedly make courageous choices while spreading goodness like it's fairy dust on sale at Costco! In* Stories *we witness Heidi living with trust and in the flow of the Universe and her relentless bid toward spreading positivity, hold us captive and inspired to do the same as we make our way on this planet.*

- Victoria Lorient-Faibish MEd, RP, CCC, BCPP, RPE
  Registered Psychotherapist, Keynote Speaker & Author of
  Find Your "Self-Culture:" Moving From Depression and Anxiety to Monumental Self-Acceptance and *Connecting: Rewire Your Relationship-Culture*

stories

finding your wings

To Tammy,
Always remember to
spread positivity & shine
your light!
Heidi

stories

finding your wings

HEIDI ALLEN

ĕß
echo
BOOKS

an imprint of
Wintertickle Press

Publication Information Available from Library and Archives Canada Cataloguing

ISBN 9781894813969

PRINTED IN CANADA

Published by Wintertickle Press
132 Commerce Park Drive, Unit K, Suite 155,
Barrie, ON L4N 0Z7

WintertucklePress.com

First and foremost, I would like to dedicate this book to my dear friend and mentor, Madelyn Hamilton. I am forever grateful for your love, your belief in me, and your incredible guidance. You never let me lose sight of my vision and were always there to remind me of it when I needed it most. Thank you for being my angel on earth.

I would also like to dedicate this book to my amazing children, Michael and Haydn. Both of you have taught me more than you will ever know. Being your mom has been my greatest gift, hardest challenge, and most treasured moments I could ever wish for. Thank you both for your love and most of all, your patience with me as I searched for my true purpose in life. I didn't always make it easy for our family and yet you never lost faith in me and did your best to always support and love me. I'm so proud of both of you and love you both so much.

Last but not least, I want to dedicate this book to my incredible husband, Mike. Without your unconditional love and encouragement, I have no idea how I would have gotten through the last number of years. As thousands of people have come to depend on me, I'm truly grateful and indebted to be able to depend on you. You are my rock of support, my best friend, and the love of my life. I can't imagine living a moment without you by my side. Thank you for always taking care of me, believing in me and loving me, but most of all, thank you for realizing I'm the most hilarious person ☺. I love you forever, Mike.

CONTENTS

Introduction — *1*
Prologue — *7*

Chapter 1: Signs — 9

A Wink from the Universe.....................................11
If You Build It.....................................17
My Jumanji.....................................21

Chapter 2: My Early Years — 29

Nana's Words.....................................31
Regret—Just Let Go.....................................38
My Tiara.....................................43

Chapter 3: Marriage — 51

You Had Me at Harry.....................................53
Marriage Is a Rainbow.....................................59
The "Right" Bench.....................................64
What a Difference Twenty-Four Hours Makes.....................................70
The Big Talk.....................................75

Chapter 4: Kids — 81

The Video Game of Life.....................................83
Everybody's Got a Story.....................................90
Family Day.....................................95
Who's Living Your Life.....................................100
Free Pass.....................................106
I Choose the Roller Coaster.....................................112
A Plague of Joy.....................................117

Chapter 5: **Friendship — 123**

You'll Never Believe Who I Heard from Today.......................125

Lucky Charms Aren't Just for Kids.................................130

I Felt Betrayed...134

A Simple Gesture...138

Chapter 6: **Life and Death — 143**

Ordinary to Extaordinary.......................................145

It Just Takes Time...149

It Made Me Feel Loved..154

86,400 Seconds...158

Chapter 7: **Experiences — 165**

Traded My Mask for a Cape......................................167

I Made a Mistake...172

A Cyclone Hits Costco..176

My War with Patience...182

Set the Odometer...188

The Five-Gallon Pot..194

Together We Can Make a Difference..............................199

INTRODUCTION

*"The two most important days of your life are the day you
were born, and the day you find out why."*
~ Mark Twain

Finding My Wings

I'm probably going to get fired if I send this text," I said to my
husband, Mike.

"That's never stopped you before," he replied.

"You're right," I responded and hit Send without hesitation.

You see, growing up, I was always an incredibly optimistic
person with big dreams to make a huge difference in the world,
and nothing ever stopped me. Yes, I realize many people feel
this way, but for me it was an overwhelming driving force, dic-
tating and controlling every life decision I made. I felt I had a
great destiny, which granted me tremendous confidence and an
unwavering need to follow my heart. I always fight for what's
right no matter the consequences.

I've abandoned incredibly successful careers, moved cities,
spent hundreds of hours learning new skills, and held more new
titles than I have fingers, never backing down and never regret-
ting a decision—all in pursuit of my great destiny. The problem
was I had no idea what my destiny actually was.

Time passed and I was working as a fashion makeover producer on a popular television show. I loved my job, but I didn't
always agree with their work ethic. Most of the time, I could

tolerate and justify it—the trade-off was that I was making a massive difference in women's lives. Yet when I was asked to turn a blind eye to something incredibly questionable, I couldn't just stand idly by anymore and accept it. However, my protest fell on deaf ears.

Not willing to let it go, I made a final appeal via the fateful text. It was a miracle I wasn't fired. Instead, a fair and right decision was made. I had won the battle, yet somehow, I had lost the war. Any enthusiasm I previously had for the production seemed to disappear after this day. I was no longer able to look the other way. My rose-coloured glasses were lost, and it was time for me to move on.

Still in love with the idea of working in television, I felt my only option was to set my sights even higher: Oprah Winfrey higher. *Go big or go home,* I thought. Determined to get her attention and a job working for her, I wrote the most awe-inspiring cover letter I'd ever written, meticulously choosing every word to prove I was unmistakably an obvious choice.

Feeling proud of my work of art, I printed the letter to make one final check for mistakes. I couldn't risk being rejected because of a simple spelling error. Yet the moment I held the letter, an uneasy, anxious feeling swept over me—a hesitation I'd never encountered before. I actually wondered if the confusing feelings were self-doubt. Did I think I couldn't get the job?

No way . . . you're a self-professed Type A personality on overdrive, and you've never failed at anything you wanted, I bragged to myself.

Then why am I hesitating? Don't I want the job? I apprehensively questioned. I sat for a few minutes, and then an overwhelming rush of emotions came over me. "Oh my God—I don't!" I gasped aloud.

It was just that fast. In one split second, my overconfident swagger had quickly turned into devastating clarity. It was an unnerving and confusing feeling. If I didn't want to work for Oprah, but I also unquestionably knew I couldn't continue working where I was, what was I supposed to do now? More importantly, who was I supposed to be?

For the first time in my life, I didn't have the answers and felt like a complete failure. It crushed me. In the months that followed, I began to isolate myself. I didn't eat, I hardly slept, and I cried continually. I had spiralled into a black hole and didn't know how to find my way out. Then like a beacon of hope, an unexpected email hit my inbox. An old friend and mentor I hadn't heard from in years asked to see me.

I was happy to hear from her but felt too depressed to meet. I decided to reply with a dismissive excuse. However, her persistent emails would eventually sway me, and I agreed to meet at her home. The moment she saw me, she knew something was wrong—even with my best attempt to hide my pain.

Before I knew it, I was confessing everything to her: the fateful text, the unsent cover letter, the devastating discovery, my confusion and sheer depression. She just listened. Three emotional hours later, my friend decided it was my turn to listen. Compassionately, she acknowledged my pain. She told me she admired my determination and tenacity and had enjoyed watching me move from one successful career to the next, always in search of my great destiny, yet never finding it. Then very directly, she admitted she always felt like I'd missed looking in one very important place.

"Where?" I asked, completely oblivious to what she was referring to.

"Inside your heart," she answered. "You've never stopped to ask yourself what you want or what your true passion is.

"This breakdown, Heidi, is no more than a gift for you to finally discover what you've always been looking for," she explained.

"I wouldn't call what I'm going through a gift," I wept, feeling very sorry for myself and deflated by her response. I also insisted I didn't even know where to start.

"Give me a minute," she answered and left the room. When she returned, she handed me a pad of paper and two blue pencils. Puzzled by the items, I asked what she expected me to do with them. "Start by getting to know yourself a little better. Make you a priority and schedule a meeting with yourself every week," she explained.

I had journalled in the past, but I was unsure of my friend's advice. Yet so desperate to feel better, I agreed to try it.

The following Wednesday I met with myself for the first time. I actually wrote non-stop for an hour. My words were raw, painful, and incredibly vulnerable. I wrote about how angry I was at myself, my job, my life, and the overwhelming pressure I felt to make a difference. I questioned my confidence, my decisions, and most of all, I questioned, *Why me?*

How is this supposed to be helping me? I cried to myself. The meeting had felt more like torture.

The following week, to avoid the same torment, I decided to eliminate any and all emotional thought. I was determined to keep it extremely professional. I created several pro/con lists, wrote about my likes and dislikes, and set numerous goals. It was a left-brain fiesta party that even my emotionally driven right brain enjoyed.

Huh. Maybe this could work, I smugly thought.

For weeks, I continued the meetings. I was able to keep some super organized, whereas others still fell off track and left me feeling emotionally weak again. Yet something was changing. I started to notice that random conversations and opportunities began feeling more like coincidental messages, each one guiding me like signposts to understand who I was and what I was meant to do.

Then, as if the answer had always been there, I knew what I was supposed to do. It was unbelievably clear, and I couldn't wait to tell someone.

"I feel I'm supposed to start a blog," I confessed to my husband.

"Really? A blog about what?" he asked, a little surprised by my announcement.

"I believe I'm meant to share my stories," I answered, feeling really sure about my path.

"Cool! You have amazing stories. What are you gonna call it?" he questioned, always being my biggest fan and supporter.

"I hadn't really thought of a name," I answered and looked down at my notepad for clues.

Surprisingly, three words immediately stood out like neon signs from random places on the paper. As I wrote the words on the bottom of the page, I said the name aloud: "Positive People Army."

My husband chuckled. "Well, I didn't expect to hear *that*. What's the Positive People Army?"

As I stared at the words, an overwhelming rush of both fear and excitement took my breath away and made my skin tingle.

"Heidi, did you hear me? What's the Positive People Army?" he asked again, trying to get my attention.

When I finally exhaled, I felt like I'd let go of a lifetime of holding my breath. It was unbelievably powerful and exhilarating. I felt awake.

"Are you okay?" Mike asked, looking a little confused by my reaction.

When I finally composed myself, I admitted to Mike I'd never been better. A few weeks later, I launched the Positive People Army blog with its first story. I still didn't understand what the PPA was, but I had faith the answers would come.

In the coming months, hundreds of people found the website. It felt amazing to connect with so many people and to make a positive difference together. I felt alive. What I've come to learn is we are not born with a perfectly clear answer as to what our purpose is. It's a struggle almost every person goes through—a struggle because we become so distracted by work, daily commitments, goals, and other people's opinions. Our awareness of our unique life purpose is easily dimmed, leaving us feeling lost, lonely, unfulfilled, and depressed.

No matter how noisy the world gets or how hard the darkness seems, we need to remember there is always a small voice whispering. That voice is you, waiting to be heard and acknowledged. Just like Glenda the Good Witch told Dorothy in *The Wizard of Oz*, "You've always had the power, my dear. You just had to learn it for yourself."

I did eventually leave my job, and the Positive People Army has grown into an incredible positive movement. All because I chose to listen to my heart and my purpose, my destiny appeared. So, I ask all of you, are you ready to listen to that voice inside you? The world is waiting to hear.

PROLOGUE

Who am I? Why am I here? What am I looking for? We all ask ourselves these questions at one time or another while navigating life. I call this finding your wings. Be it courage, confidence, happiness, passion, or strength, finding your wings is whatever you are looking for in life. Yet where do you even begin?

For some of you, you have spent a lifetime seeking these answers, always looking outside yourself, denying your own intuition, emotions, and opinion. Accumulating a wealth of knowledge and experience in so many areas but never realizing you always had the answers within.

Stories: Finding Your Wings is my multicoloured personal journey to finding my own wings. An extremely colourful and unconventional expedition, wrought with mistakes, setbacks, and even a breakdown. All in pursuit of my wings—the Positive People Army.

My hope is that as you read my stories, they will empower and inspire you to navigate your own life to discover the answers buried deep inside you. Take a moment after each story to answer the questions that follow it. Open your mind and search back through your memories, experiences, tragedies, and treasures to find what it is you're searching for. Remember, all that you seek has always been seeking you, too.

Are you ready to discover your wings?

CHAPTER 1

Signs

S ome of my greatest lessons didn't come from books or school, but from the universe itself. You may have heard the saying "everything happens for a reason." Well, I believe nothing could be truer! Have you ever been thinking of something and notice the song lyrics playing on the radio reflect your thoughts? A random conversation leads you to an answer you were seeking, or maybe you keep bumping into the same stranger over and over? This is likely a universal sign.

Throughout this chapter I share stories filled with subtle signs, winks, and coincidences, each one bringing me guidance and answers I'd been asking for. So the next time you really notice something, think about what made you notice it and why. Chances are, it's a sign sent just for you!

"The universe is always speaking to us . . .
Sending us little messages, causing coincidences and
serendipities, reminding us to stop, to look around, to believe
in something else, something more."
~ Anonymous

A Wink from the Universe

Things work out perfectly sometimes—like when you arrive at the platform just as your train is pulling into the station, or when you have the exact change in your pocket for the parking meter, or when you're standing in line at the grocery store and you meet your future husband. Stuff like that. Right place, right time.

Change one tiny element and your whole life might be completely different. For a fleeting moment, we feel like something special occurred like fate or serendipity. Of course, we inevitably brush it off as chance or coincidence. But when such an event saves your life, it gets a little bit more difficult to call it blind luck, like during my first year of university when I found myself in the wrong place at the right time.

My relationship with my mother was strained, to put it diplomatically. It often felt like constant arguments and relentless tension with only enough respite in between so we could catch our breath for the next round. After years of tolerating her guilt trips and ridicule, the last straw came when she issued me an ultimatum. It was either her way or the highway. I chose the highway, as anyone who knows me could easily predict.

That very night, as I left the house with everything I owned, she vowed to never speak to me again. *No problem*, I thought. At last, we saw eye to eye on something. But despite my bravado, for the first time in my life I felt lost, alone, and confused. It was an emptiness I'd never felt before. In an attempt to escape these new sensations, I agreed to take a road trip to Nova Scotia with my boyfriend. Somehow, we scraped together just enough cash to do so, and with a car full of snacks, mixed tapes, and youthful hope, we rode east on the open road. It's hard not to think about your problems during a twenty-four-hour ride in a cramped two-seater, but I did my best.

Once we arrived, I successfully managed to forget all the problems waiting for me back home. For one blissful week, we visited his family members, took in the beauty of the province, and indulged in all the east coast food and drink we could handle. I loved every minute of it.

The day we left, the weather was beautiful. As I sat in the passenger seat and stared out the window, I couldn't stop thinking about all the great times I'd had over the last week: dancing with my boyfriend's uncles at a down east kitchen party, devouring so much fresh seafood our stomachs hurt, hiking stunning scenic trails that took my breath away. I hadn't felt this way in a long time—happy. But as night fell, the weather changed and my mood with it.

Seemingly out of nowhere, a dense fog appeared and cloaked the road in a thick veil of grey. Very quickly, the world felt dark and desolate. Our headlights stabbed out into nothing. We were alone in the world. Silence filled the car, the fog having smothered the conversation as surely as it had smothered the light. Now, with no distractions, all I could think about was my situation back home. Did I make the right decision moving out? Would I ever speak to my mom again? Could I ever shake this feeling of emptiness and loneliness? I suddenly felt so sad and— BANG! I was rudely startled out of my rumination.

"I can't control the car!" my boyfriend yelled, desperately trying to steer.

"What's happening?" I screamed as the car swerved and drifted sideways. The tires screeched. Rocks, dust, and dirt swirled all around us.

"Brace yourself!" he yelled.

I'm going to die, I thought.

We came to an abrupt stop, a cloud of dust settling around us, a friend of the fog.

My boyfriend was slumped over the steering wheel.

"Are you okay?" I asked, my voice trembling and frantic.

"Yes. I'm pretty sure we blew a tire," he mumbled.

I breathed a sigh of relief. But it seemed our troubles weren't quite over yet.

"I don't have a spare. I just replaced these tires so I took the extra tire out to fit our baggage into the trunk."

"What are we going to do? We're in the middle of nowhere," I said, panicked and scared. I looked out the window, but the fog held no answers.

"I have no idea," he snapped. He opened his door and walked to the front of the car.

I joined him. We sat on the hood in silence.

"Maybe once it gets light out we can flag a car down to help."

He nodded "yes." The silence remained unchallenged.

"Are you guys okay?" a voice suddenly asked from behind us.

Startled, we screamed and jumped off the hood, turning to confront our murderer.

"I'm so sorry! I didn't mean to scare you," the equally startled stranger explained.

"Oh my God! Where did you come from?!" I shrieked.

"Nowhere," he answered cryptically, "but I'm heading to the next town. Did you want me to call a tow truck for you?"

"Yes, that would be great," I said. Though I was starting to feel relieved, I still wasn't convinced this man wasn't going to pull out a machete or something. It was an odd mix of emotions.

"Don't worry. You're safe now." He smiled and then turned and disappeared into the fog.

Baffled by his unexplained appearance (and disappearance), we did the only thing we could: stare at each other in silent disbelief.

Fifteen minutes later, two streams of light sliced through the fog and found us by the side of the road. It didn't seem possible. The next exit was over forty minutes away by car. How did that peculiar stranger get there so quickly? This night had gone from beautiful to scary to weird.

"Blew a tire, I heard," the tow truck driver yelled as he walked towards us.

"Yes, we did."

"It was a pretty lucky coincidence, if you ask me," he remarked.

"Excuse me?" I replied, confused.

"You didn't hear about the pileup?"

"What pileup?"

"The fog is so thick past the next exit, it caused a massive car pileup. If you didn't blow your tire, you probably would have ended up in that crash."

I shuddered at the thought. Who knows what would have happened to us? Wrong place, right time.

Before long, the tire had been fixed and we were back on the road again. Hundreds of miles later, I still couldn't stop thinking about what had just happened.

I had never really paid much attention to coincidences. Like most people, I'd dismissed them as chance or luck. But this felt like so much more to me. I felt like I'd personally been given a wink from the universe, and I just couldn't ignore it.

The fog lifted that day and so did my feelings of confusion and loneliness. I'd been so upset, wondering if I would ever speak to my mom again, and, without that tire blowing, I may never have gotten the opportunity. The fog and the tire, two seemingly unrelated coincidences, had come together and created a life-changing moment for me.

My relationship with my mom has never been easy, but I did make up with her once I returned from that trip. And from that day forward, I paid much more attention to these "random" unexplained moments: a phone call from a long-lost friend I'd been thinking about, a timely financial windfall when I needed it most, a seemingly random meeting at a social event that led to the perfect job opportunity—simple, amazing moments that together create something complex and beautiful to guide me through this crazy life.

To quote one of my favourite authors, Paulo Coelho, "Coincidence is the language of the stars. For something to happen, so many forces have to be put into action."

The way I look at it, the universe is always trying to guide us, always trying to speak to us. We have the choice if we want to listen. I've got my ear pressed close to the ground. Do you?

Questions: A Wink from the Universe

Take a moment to think about the universal winks that have shown up in your own life, then answer the following questions to help give you some more clarity.

Do you believe in universal winks?

When you are on the right path, little coincidences can often occur in the form of synchronicity. Think back to moments throughout your earlier years where this may have occurred. What was the sign, and how did it help guide you?

How did it feel to receive the signs?

Coincidences and signs are shown to us continually. The same numbers appear, déjà vu occurs, or random conversations hold the answers you are looking for. Take a moment to list all the synchronicities occurring in your life today. Do you know why they are happening?

Are the signs scaring you, or are you ready to receive them? Why?

> "Sometimes the questions are complicated and
> the answers are simple."
> ~ Dr. Seuss

If You Build It . . .

Signs are all around us. They can be as subtle as a whisper or as blatant as a slap in the face. They can be spelled out on the news or suggested in the clouds. They're in the stories we read and in the songs we hear. Some say it's all just coincidence, but I believe that signs are real. They're out there and waiting to be read by anyone with an open mind and an open heart. We just need to make sure we're paying enough attention to notice them.

I've seen many signs in my life. Some were small, some were life changing, and some were both—like the sign I saw towards the end of my first marriage. For a long time, it had been clear to us that we were going to separate. It was coming as surely as the tide. In one last-ditch effort, my husband suggested we take a Caribbean vacation to see if there was anything left to save. Having a hard time dealing with the apparent end of our marriage, I agreed to take the trip.

For a week we relaxed and tried to reconnect. To my surprise, I actually started to enjoy his company again. Sitting next to him on the beach, staring out at the glistening water, a long-dormant optimism began to bloom inside of me.

But no amount of paradise could silence the nagging questions swirling through my mind: Could I really make this marriage work? Could I really be happy? Was this warm feeling the rekindling of passion or just the Caribbean sun on my skin? However, in the end it was my optimism that won, and as I boarded the plane, I actually thought to myself, *Yes, I can make this work.*

An hour into the flight, I decided to watch the movie *Serendipity*, starring John Cusack and Kate Beckinsale. I love John Cusack, of course, so I was thrilled that the movie was available. I couldn't have known I was about to see so much more than just a feel-good romantic comedy. I was about to see a sign.

As the plot unfolded, something incredible happened. I felt like the movie was talking to me directly. In the flick, John Cusack realizes he needs to make the difficult choice to leave his fiancée, because he knows his true love is out there and that he shouldn't settle. It was just the slap in the face I needed. As the movie ended, I couldn't control my tears. I knew in that moment, without a doubt, that my marriage was over. It was a tough message to hear, but it's what forced me to realize that in order to be truly happy, I needed to make an extremely difficult decision. I needed to end my marriage. A few weeks later, I did just that.

Flash-forward: Much like John Cusack, I ended up finding my true love, and we've been happily married for over fourteen years. My husband says that *Serendipity* is one of his favourite movies, if only for the reason that he wouldn't have met me without it. He can be very charming.

Recently, another movie gave me a sign. During my journey to figure out how I was going to make a bigger difference in life, I noticed that one of my favourite movies was playing on TV: *Field of Dreams* with Kevin Costner. The film's iconic line, "If you build it, he will come," resonated deeply with me that day. It actually gave me goosebumps!

For days, I couldn't get the line out of my head. One morning while brushing my teeth, the line suddenly morphed into "If you build it, they will come." It stopped me dead in my tracks. I stared at myself, wide-eyed in the bathroom mirror. This was a sign. And right then, the idea to create a Facebook group for Positive People Army struck me. Now the group has thousands of people interacting from all over the world. The Positive People Army is growing, and it's making a difference! I opened my mind and heart, and the signs were revealed to me.

Questions: If You Build It . . .

When you were going through a difficult time in the past, did you ever notice some subtle or blatantly obvious signs you were given? List each one to remind yourself how you are continually guided.

What are you struggling with at the moment? Your job/career, a relationship, health concerns? Have you noticed any signs showing up trying to guide you? List any and all signals you've received.

Do you need to make a decision about something in your life? If so, what is it?

What answer(s) are you hoping to receive? Be honest with yourself.

How does it make you feel to admit that you need to make a decision?

What can you do today to move yourself closer to making a decision?

Are you ready to make the decision? If not, why?

> "Coincidence is God's way of staying anonymous."
> ~ Albert Einstein

My Jumanji

A year after I launched the Positive People Army blog, including a few months growing the PPA Facebook Group, I began wondering if the PPA was the destiny I'd always searched for. It wasn't that anything had gone wrong, it was just a moment of doubt.

Mike and I were leaving for a trip to Cuba, so I decided to distract myself from my uncertain thoughts and find a book for the trip. While perusing the self-help section, one particular book title immediately caught my attention. It read "When God Winks: How the Power of Coincidence Guides Your Life."

Huh, I thought.

As I've mentioned earlier, I have a strong belief in signs and messages. I call them universal winks, but I'd never actually thought about these occurrences as direct messages from God. Now I'm not saying I don't have faith in God; I do. I'd just never considered the winks or coincidences to be divinely sent.

I decided to investigate the intriguing book further by reading the inside front cover:

"It is not by accident that you just picked up *When God Winks*. Whether you call it synchronicity or coincidence, what brought you to this book today is worth remembering. In fact, you may have suspected all along that there is more to coincidence than meets the eye. These seemingly random events are actually signposts that can help you successfully navigate your career, relationships, and interests. [Author] SQuire Rushnell shows us that by recognizing our 'God Winks,' we can use the untapped power of coincidence to vastly improve our lives."

Are you kidding me? Did this book just speak to me? I thought, feeling a little creeped out. I quickly closed the book and returned it to the shelf.

Yet I couldn't stop staring at it. I almost felt like I'd just stumbled upon my own version of Jumanji and I could hear it calling to me. In the end I finally gave in to the mysterious book and bought it.

On my first day in Cuba I found myself just staring at the book again. Unable to open it.

What is wrong with me? I thought. *It's just a book. If you don't like it, you don't have to read it.*

My pep talk seemed to work because I finally turned to page one and began reading. I immediately became fascinated with the author's theory that coincidences weren't just happenstances, but God's response to our thoughts and questions. It seemed unbelievable. Yet page after page, my belief was increasing by the strong evidence that had played out in history, sports, medicine, and relationships.

I was also captivated by how each new chapter triggered my own coincidental memories. I was starting to believe in the possibility that an omnipresent force could have created the synchronicities.

It was mind-blowing.

Lying in the sun on my last vacation day, I sadly finished the book and closed my eyes, the author's last words repeating in my mind: "From now on, whenever a coincidence pops up at a particularly auspicious moment in your life, I hope you will come to say, 'I wonder. Was that a God Wink?' Chances are good that it was."

So I wondered. Was picking up the book my God Wink? After sitting with the question for what felt like hours, I finally mustered up enough nerve to walk to the beach and ask God himself.

"Hello, God. It's me, Heidi," I began.

I then continued by expressing my sincerest gratitude for bringing me the book. I also spoke about my plans for the Positive People Army and asked that he confirm whether I'm on the right path with some clear winks—some specific coincidences that would help me believe the PPA is my destiny.

What happened next was awe inspiring!

An hour before we were to leave the resort, I sat outside and watched as dark clouds quickly rolled in and a torrential tropical downpour started. Mike frantically ran to grab the bags waiting outside for the bus, but all I could do was stand in disbelief.

You see, one year ago, almost to the date, we had also vacationed in Cuba, and exactly one hour before we left during that trip, a violent downpour had also occurred. Just like the one I was witnessing now.

Was this a wink? I thought to myself. It just felt so subtle. More like a whisper and not so much a clear sign. I decided to look up and say thank you anyway.

Now on the plane home I couldn't stop thinking about the rainstorm, and I hoped my next sign would be a little more precise and clear. Eventually my thoughts wandered and I became distracted by the in-flight movie. The flick was about halfway through when an announcement interrupted it. The flight staff were looking for a particular family and asked politely for the "Squire family" to make themselves known.

"Oh my God," I said aloud and placed my hand over my mouth.

My husband grabbed my leg and asked if I was okay.

"Did you hear the name they asked for?" I said with an excited shake in my voice.

"I'm pretty sure they said the Squire family. Why?" he asked, a little confused.

"Mike, that's the author's name of *When God Winks*. His name is SQuire Rushnell. Isn't it incredible? That was a wink . . . a pretty big wink!" I answered.

The rain may or may not have been a wink, but there was no denying this synchronistic moment had been cleverly orchestrated for me to recognize it as a true sign. I felt giddy with excitement and yet overwhelmed at the same time. It just felt so unbelievable. How could God be directly speaking to me?

I spent the rest of the flight talking with my husband about my miracle and how grateful I was for the answer. I felt so privileged to have a personal audience with a higher power. Once we landed, however, my exhilaration was quickly crushed when we were detained by customs and ushered into another room for questioning. *Don't they know who I was in personal contact with?* I thought to myself.

The customs agent began the interview with some pretty routine questions: our full names, why and where we had travelled, and our home address, which we graciously gave.

"Are you kidding me?" the agent asked when I gave our address.

"I'm sorry?" I said, a little puzzled.

"I grew up on that street!" she enthusiastically responded.

"Unbelievable," I declared and started to laugh.

Unbeknownst to her, the significance of this incredible happenstance wasn't just a random coincidence but had been divinely sent. My heart filled with such gratitude.

Forty-five minutes later we were finally told we'd been released without an explanation. Incredibly confused, my husband inquired why they had questioned us.

"Mistaken identity," the agent remarked.

"In what way?" Mike asked.

"Sir, you actually have the exact same full name and birthdate as a wanted criminal," she explained.

"No way!" I blurted out, looking at Mike, who was shaking his head in complete disbelief.

"Now that was a wink!" I exclaimed out loud.

To this day, I'm still in awe of what happened. From a subtle whispered wink to a coincidence that felt like it was being screamed from the top of a mountain, I have no doubt in my mind I was being directly spoken to.

The way I see it, the universe or the divine—whichever you believe—is always speaking to us. Sending us little messages, causing coincidences and serendipities. Reminding us to stop, to look around, and to believe in something else, something more. Instead of ignoring or fighting it and always trying to figure things out on your own, I suggest you just ask and then wait for your incredible winks to appear.

Because they always do . . . when you're listening.

Questions: My Jumanji

When I decided to write this book, I questioned whether I should share this particular story. My mission with the PPA is to always keep things as neutral as possible. However, my faith in God means a lot to me, and I felt if I didn't share my faith, then I wasn't truly being my authentic self. If you are uncomfortable with the story and my beliefs, please feel free to skip these questions. I will not be offended.

Have you ever felt like you've had a divine intervention? A moment when you felt God was personally speaking to you?

Did you believe it, or did you fluff it off as something else?

How did it make you feel to receive a message from God?

Is there something you would like to ask God now? What is it?

Are you ready to ask a question of God? If not, why?

Some people struggle with or have abandoned their faith because of a traumatic background or tragedy. It is understandable. If this is you, what would it take for you to ask a question and keep an open mind to receive an answer?

CHAPTER 2

My Early Years

You get more flies with honey than with vinegar; always say please and thank you; don't talk to strangers; look both ways before you cross—these are just a few of the many pieces of advice I was given growing up. Timeless wisdom passed down from generation to generation.

However, life is so much more than what is taught to us. It's our experiences, relationships, and perspectives that shape and mould us into the people we become. The next few stories are special teachable moments that helped me change the course of my life.

Wishing you a great trip down memory lane.

"Journaling is like whispering to one's self and
listening at the same time."
~ Mina Murray, Dracula

Nana's Words

Words have always felt pretty powerful to me. When you think about it, without words, a thought can never become a reality. Written, spoken, or read, one or two specifically chosen words can cause people to fall in love or painfully break their hearts. With one simple phrase, a person's life can be changed forever.

For me, my love of words started pretty early. My eighth birthday to be exact. I tore open my nana's gift to reveal a small blue and white book with a young girl on the cover and the word DIARY spelled out in large blue letters. I looked up at her and asked, "What's a diary?"

She smiled and explained, "It's a precious book where you can write about all the fun things you did throughout your day. Think of it as a beautiful book for your eyes only. A place to keep all your secrets as well as your wishes and dreams to help them come true."

Her words felt so magical that day, and I did just as she asked. I filled my diary with secret crushes, Barbie dreams, and hopes for what I would be when I grew up. My diary became one of my most treasured possessions.

You see, my nana was pretty incredible like that. At only five-foot-one, with brilliant white hair and the most infectious laugh, she always made me feel so special. I was the first grandchild, born the day after her birthdate—we had an extraordinary unspoken bond that made us inseparable at times. I loved and admired her deeply.

On my thirteenth birthday, my nana purchased another diary for me. A red leather-bound book with a heart-shaped lock and key. The smell and touch of the leather reminded me of a book you'd find in an old English library. It made me feel so grown up.

Once again, she encouraged me to write. However, this time she urged me to embrace the young woman I was becoming. She told me to write from the heart and to not be afraid of the changes and emotions I would go through. It was incredible how important her advice would become as I navigated the next few awkward years.

Entries were no longer filled with childlike hopes and dreams. I was now using the book to help me through my uncomfortable pubescent years. Anything from dramatic body changes to embarrassing moments, like buying my first bra, to the tragic ups and downs of adolescent love. Arguments with my parents, friendship drama, my ever-changing celebrity crushes. Unbeknownst to me, this simple writing habit was helping me to truly understand myself.

I continued this emotional practice for most of my high school years. Yet as I got ready for university and became busier with school, friends, and a part-time job, the practice fell by the wayside.

Flash-forward to my early thirties and the end of my first marriage. I started writing again. However, writing would take on a new form. Remembering my nana's words, I started writing from my heart once more. No longer called a diary but a journal, the pages had become more like my own personal therapist.

Some days I wrote about my anger and frustration, whereas others days I couldn't stop myself from reminiscing and crying about what went wrong. It was a painful and raw documentation to say the least. Being able to purge my emotions was becoming my saving grace. In fact, eventually my pain and heartache subsided, and I was able to forgive and let go of all the pain.

Over the years I've owned many journals, each one specifically used to help me through a difficult time or emotional crossroad in my life. I've even shared in this book how journalling once a week helped me discover my life's purpose—the Positive People Army. Yet for some reason, once the PPA was formed my journal entries seemed to change. They were no longer emotionally driven but were more focused on only my plans, goals, and ideas. I could sense something felt missing but quickly dismissed the feelings and became more determined to try to figure out what the PPA was and what I was supposed to be doing.

Yet the universe had other plans for me in the form of a getaway girlfriend weekend at a magical place called Grail Springs, a beautiful retreat location up north, promising only rest and rejuvenation. The offer was something I couldn't resist.

As luck would have it, the day we arrived I noticed a class was being offered on journalling. Thrilled, I jumped at the opportunity to gain any new clarity and signed us all up. However, sitting in the class that afternoon, I felt extremely uncomfortable. Every time the instructor spoke, it seemed like she was speaking directly to me, like I was the only person in the group. Every scenario she mentioned felt familiar. Her examples were similar to my own situation, and she seemed to answer each and every question I'd ever had about journalling.

It was hard to believe this was just coincidental. Yet the most eerie part of the afternoon was when she looked directly at me and started instructing me to not just ask for the answers, but to intend them. She also told me I needed to clearly state with specific details what my success was supposed to look like, to feel like, and how I wanted it to happen to ensure it would come to fruition. The entire explanation was weird. I hadn't asked her for any advice and yet, somehow, she was responding to me as if I had.

Confused, I looked around the room to see if anyone else had noticed what had just occurred. Yet nobody seemed to notice her directness with me or even question what had happened.

Even though I was a little shaken by the odd experience, I decided I would take her advice anyway. *What have I got to lose?* I thought. That night, I wrote page after page of intentions for my family, my health, and the future of the Positive People Army. In one particular paragraph, I even wrote about my intentions to become a public speaker. I described my desire to be in front of a large audience and my dream to be able to influence people on a grand scale.

As I fell asleep that night, I couldn't help but get excited to see what would happen next. If the advice rang true, my life was about to get really interesting.

Not even twenty-four hours later, I was stunned to realize one of my intentions was actually coming true. It was hard to believe, but during a conversation with a colleague, she offered me a speaking engagement job in front of a large audience of around two thousand people.

I felt like I'd just found a magic lamp and made a wish, and a magic genie was miraculously granting it for me. I was giddy with excitement. However, my enthusiasm wouldn't last long. As she explained the event details, I suddenly realized she wanted me to speak about my television and media experience.

This wasn't what I intended, I thought—or was it?

After everything I'd been through, I knew in my heart I no longer wished to pursue opportunities in the television industry. Yes, I knew a lot on the subject, but I wasn't willing to sell out and speak on it for the sake of speaking in front of a large audience. I knew I only wanted to speak on topics that would inspire and motivate people.

So what went wrong? I asked myself. I was incredibly confused.

When I was able, I immediately re-read my journal entry—especially the paragraph about speaking—yet nothing seemed to jump out at me. Frustrated, I threw the journal on the floor, lay back on the bed, and closed my eyes, searching my brain for any clues about how I could've screwed up.

Moments later, like a neon sign pulsating in a shop window, a word leapt forward in my thoughts. The word was *specific*.

"Oh my God, was I specific enough?" I blurted and jumped up to grab my journal from the floor. This time I read the paragraph aloud. Focusing on every word as if my life depended on it. Making sure I comprehended exactly what I'd asked for.

When I finished reading, I placed the book on the bed and just stared at my words, awestruck by what I'd just discovered. Yes, I had intended to become a speaker, but what I'd left out was one very important and SPECIFIC detail: what I wanted to speak about. I was dumbfounded and actually started to giggle.

Yet again, words and writing had proven their incredible power to me.

Throughout the years, it's amazing how my writing has taken on many styles. Whether it was to discover myself, de-clutter my mind, heal from heartache, or affirm my future, words and journalling have always been there for me. Writing is my friend when I need to vent, a therapist to help me work through my emotions, and a guide to help me process and break down complex situations. It's one thing to live your life, but without taking the time to observe, reflect, grow, and let go, we can never fully understand all we're supposed to learn.

It's been years now since my beautiful nana passed away, and I often wonder what she would say about my journalling experiences and discoveries. Deep down, I have a feeling she would only encourage me to keep writing.

And I hope you are inclined to do the same.

Questions: Nana's Words

Do you remember having a diary as a kid? Did it help you?

What is your fondest memory of writing in your diary?

Did you continue writing, or did you give it up? What age did you stop?

Do you know why you stopped writing?

Do you journal as an adult?

Why did you start journalling again?

How has journal writing helped you?

If you don't journal, why not?

After reading how journalling has helped me so much, are you considering journal writing?

> "Never regret anything because at one time it was
> exactly what you wanted."
> ~ Anonymous

Regret—Just Let Go

There's a recurring theme in the quotes my friend has been posting on Facebook lately: regret. Her latest post read, "I don't regret my past, I just regret the time I wasted with the wrong people."

I assumed she was talking about her ex-husband, who had hurt and humiliated her. Recovering from that relationship had been a hard process. A process that wasn't over, it seemed. Even years later, she still carried the emotional burden of regret. How long can someone shoulder that weight before their knees buckle?

Many years ago, I had found myself in a similar state. During my senior years of high school, I worked part time for a nursing agency, visiting the elderly in their homes and helping them with personal care, light housekeeping, and things like that. Other times I was asked to work as relief staff in a nursing home, which I really enjoyed because of all the fascinating characters I met there. There were many veterans who shared riveting war stories, men and women who'd lived through times I'd only read about, and even a lady who claimed to be one of the last remaining survivors of the *Titanic*. It was a rewarding job to have at such a young age.

After I graduated high school, I decided to take a year off and work full time. With how well work was going, I thought I might not even go to university. After a few months on the job, I was starting to feel like I was part of the regular nursing home staff, and they offered me a full-time position. The offer was overwhelming. The money was more than I'd ever imagined making. It felt like a dream—a union job with benefits and vacation pay. Thinking I was set for life, I enthusiastically accepted the position.

I loved my new job. I counted the days until my three-month probation was over so I could receive my official paperwork. But two weeks before that could happen, fate intervened and sent my life on a completely different path. While trying to help a nurse lift a patient into a wheelchair, I somehow wrenched my back.

I thought I was fine, but by the end of my shift I could hardly move. I was in excruciating pain and decided to go to the emergency room. Thankfully, the doctor told me it wasn't too serious, but he ordered me to take a week off work to rest. So that's what I did, and one week later I returned to work with a bounce in my step.

During my morning break, my manager asked me to her office. *I was finally going to receive my formal documents*, I thought. I was wrong.

"Heidi, I'm sorry, but I'm going to have to terminate you," she said sadly.

Her words shocked me. I felt like I couldn't catch my breath.

She explained that receiving an injury before my probation period ended meant I was a medical risk. So this would be my last shift.

I was miserable for weeks. I played the injury over and over again in my mind. Why had I been so careless? Regret consumed me.

After being unemployed for weeks, I eventually had to take a waitressing job. I hoped keeping busy would help numb the sting of regret. It didn't.

Then one Sunday afternoon, when I was feeling my lowest, one of the nurses I had previously worked with came into the restaurant with her family. I ducked behind a wall, hoping she hadn't seen me. Feeling panicked, I asked another waitress to take her table so I wouldn't have to see her. She was swamped and couldn't help me out.

Out of options, I had to face my fear. I took a deep breath, emerged from behind the wall, and walked to my former co-worker's table. The moment she saw me she jumped up and hugged me, asking how I was doing.

"Feeling pretty low," I told her. "I haven't been great since I lost my job," I explained.

She looked puzzled for a moment. Then with a reassuring smile, she grabbed my shoulders and said, "Heidi, you never belonged at the nursing home. Fate stepped in to make sure you didn't stay there. Getting fired was actually a blessing. You're such a smart girl who can do anything you want to do . . . now go and figure out what that is."

I was dumbfounded. How did she see something that I didn't? For days I couldn't stop thinking about what she had said to me. Then one week later, with her words in my heart, I drove to my hometown university and started the application process.

I haven't looked back since, and I've never forgotten her profound words. It turns out she was right. There really was more for me out there, and I'm so thankful that fate, or whatever you want to call it, gave me the opportunity to discover that.

Since then I've come to believe that everything does happen for a reason. The people we meet, the things that happen, even the misfortunes that befall us. Good or bad, it's all part of a bigger plan.

Had I not injured my back, my life today would be drastically, unimaginably different. That sadness and regret was a difficult time in my life, but without that hard lesson I wouldn't be the person I am today.

To my lovely friend who is still feeling some regret, I offer up this quote for your wall. "Don't stare at the closed door too long—you'll miss the window opening."

Take it from me. I almost did.

Questions: Regret—Just Let Go

What is your biggest regret in life and why?

Do you believe fate had anything to do with your regret?

Could you have acted any differently considering the particular stage in your life and the information or experiences you had until that point in your life?

Are you ready to let go of your regret? If not, why?

Sometimes people are drowning in regret because they self-blame and take all the responsibility for the mistake or setback that occurred. Is your regret based on something you alone did, or was there anything or anyone else who contributed to the mistake? What would you like to say to them?

In some situations, asking questions can help you see things in a more objective manner. Try asking yourself what advice you would give to someone who is experiencing a lot of regret and blaming themselves for a situation.

What is one action you could do today to let go of regret?

"It's not what you are that is holding you back.
It's what you think you are not.
~ Anonymous

My Tiara

Over the years I've had many careers. I've owned a wedding gown store, co-hosted a radio show, and been a TV personality and producer. I've enjoyed each of them, but I always held a special place in my heart for my first career as a professional wedding photographer. I truly loved being a photographer and being a part of someone's special wedding day.

It's been more years than I can count since I've shot weddings professionally. However, I still have a keen interest in photography. In fact, I follow many photography Instagram accounts. From amateur photographers to professionals, I love looking at images captured in the moment or from faraway places I've never travelled to.

A friend of mine has a similar interest and follows some of the same accounts I do. The only difference: this particular friend is an avid traveller and has taken hundreds of beautiful photos. He really is very talented. Having returned from another adventurous trip, he shared some of his latest photos. Blown away by the images, I asked him why he hadn't started his own Instagram account of shots.

"It's hard to start an account when there are already so many photography travel pages with thousands of followers," he explained. "What if I don't get any followers, or worse what if people don't like my shots?"

"Yet how will you ever know if you don't try?" I asked.

He just shrugged and quickly changed the subject.

Later that day I thought about my friend's words and realized I knew his feelings well. The sharp sting of self-doubt. You see, when I was ten years old, I took guitar lessons at the Royal Conservatory of Music. I can't remember a chord to this day, but regardless, I did enjoy the classes.

During one of my classes, my teacher announced there was a music festival planned for all the conservatory schools in the area. Along with the music competitions being held, there were also a few other fun activities we could sign up for. They had a baking challenge, a singing contest, and even a beauty pageant. She then handed us all a colourful flyer and encouraged us to participate in as much as possible.

When I showed my mother the leaflet, she was extremely excited—especially about the beauty pageant. Without any discussion, she signed me up for the beauty contest and a guitar competition in my age group.

I objected immediately, arguing that I was never going to be beauty pageant material. Not to mention, I'd been taking guitar lessons for only a year and wasn't anywhere close to being competition ready. Yet my mother wasn't hearing any of it.

However, my grandparents, who were visiting from England at the time, seemed to sense my panic. I'd always been pretty close with both of them, so it didn't surprise me when they offered to help. Realizing I didn't seem to have a choice, I gave in and accepted my grandparents' offer.

Immediately my wonderful nana, a seamstress, took it upon herself to design and sew a pretty new dress for me to sashay down the runway in, while my grandfather put together a practice schedule for me to learn a new guitar solo. He also helped me write a short speech to address the pageant crowd and judges.

After weeks of preparation, festival day arrived. I was feeling pretty good about the guitar solo. I'd diligently followed my grandfather's schedule to a T. I actually even enjoyed the hours of practising and didn't mind my fingers callousing to look like a seasoned musician.

I'd also had fun memorizing my speech my grandfather had helped me write for the beauty contest. I wrote about being the eldest in my family, my love for skipping and hopscotch, and playing the guitar for my two cats, Pippen and Pepper. It was charming and really cute.

To prepare for the beauty contest, my mother curled my hair with hot rollers and let me put on some pink lip gloss, and my nana helped me get dressed in the white lace sundress with tiny pink tulips. I still wasn't thrilled about participating in the beauty contest, but at least I felt I looked pretty.

Once we all arrived at the festival Convention Centre, my grandfather walked me to the conference room where all the beauty contestants were to meet. The volume in the room was deafening. Pretty girls were excitedly chatting and running around the room, while a tall blonde woman was yelling, trying to get everyone's attention.

After checking me at the front table, my grandfather kissed me on the forehead and told me to have fun. I agreed I would. Yet as soon as he went to leave I grabbed his hand and begged him not to make me do the contest.

"You'll be fine, Heidi," my grandfather reassured. "Just believe in yourself . . . I know I do." He then affectionately kissed the top of my head again and disappeared through the door.

Realizing I had no choice in the matter, I walked over to where the blonde woman was directing everyone to gather. Once I sat down, I tried to replay my grandfather's words in my head, but my stomach was turning and swirling with what could only be described as a hundred butterflies flying around. My mouth was dry, my palms were clammy, and I felt a bead of sweat run down my temple. I was a nervous wreck.

"Welcome, girls," the woman bellowed. "I'm going to call out your names, and I would like everyone to line up in alphabetical order to walk to the stage.

"Once there, the MC will call your name. Please walk up to the microphone and say your full name, what city you are from, and the instrument you play. Then you will walk the runway, returning to the line until everyone has had a turn," she instructed.

Only say your name, city, and instrument . . . I prepared a speech, I thought to myself.

All of a sudden, my insane nervousness quickly turned into panicked thoughts.

If I say the speech, the blonde woman could get mad at me.
The other girls are probably going to laugh at me.
The judges may disqualify me for breaking the rules.

Stomach butterflies were no longer my concern as a sick, nauseous feeling overtook me. I even thought about running out the exit door on the other side of the stage before anyone noticed I was gone.

"Ladies and gentleman . . . welcome!" the MC announced.

Too late. I panicked, realizing I had no other choice but to do this.

As the pageant began I listened intently to the girls ahead. Each one recited only their full name, the city they lived in, and the instrument they played. Not one girl said anything more or anything less. Especially not a prepared speech!

"Heidi," the MC called out.

"Oh God. I don't want to do this," I mumbled to myself.

Walking up to the microphone I could feel my legs shaking. Fear and doubt were fully in the driver's seat now.

Then with a shake in my voice I said, "My name is Heidi Ceci. I live in St. Catharines, and I play the guitar."

Nothing more . . . and nothing less.

Yet as I returned to the back of the stage, I felt something I didn't expect. I no longer felt nervous or panicked, but guilty and ashamed of myself. Worse than that, I also felt like I'd disappointed my grandparents.

Then to make matters worse, the girl directly behind me walked up to the microphone and actually said a speech. Her name was Jennifer, and she delighted everyone with her description of her new bike, her love for chocolate ice cream, and her favourite songs she liked to play on the piano. I just stared at her in complete disbelief.

As she walked back to stand beside me, I also couldn't help but notice the blonde leader didn't tell her off, and no one seemed to be judging her for doing something different. In fact, they applauded louder for her than any other girl. And the applause continued when she stood downstage with the winning tiara on her head.

I realize there was no guarantee that if I had said my speech I would have won the beauty competition that day, but I didn't even try. I had let thoughts of doubt and fear fill my head and paralyze me. Worse than that, I had let uncertainty rob me from showing that auditorium who I truly was.

The way I see it, we have the choice to sit on the sidelines of our lives. Letting fear and doubt rule our decisions. Taking the easy road and never really trying. Yet if we push past our fears, take chances, and show the world our authentic selves, we can only ever succeed.

I may not have won the beauty contest that day, but in life I feel like I'm winning the war against fear and self-doubt every day by choosing to show up, step up, and wear my tiara of life proudly.

Are you ready to accept your crown?

Questions: My Tiara

Was there an early moment in your life when you remember yourself struggling with self-doubt?

Do you still struggle with self-doubt today? If so, when does it happen most?

How do you react when self-doubt occurs? Do you have a tendency to quit or give up?

When you suffer from self-doubt, do you find you've created stories that contribute to it? For example, I had made up stories about the blonde woman being mad at me, the girls laughing, and the judges disqualifying me.

Negative thoughts, worry, and stress can easily take on a personality of their own late at night when your brain is relaxed. Yet what we don't realize is these types of thoughts can wreak havoc on your conscience and create self-doubt. Are these types of thoughts keeping you up at night? What are these thoughts?

Are you feeling self-doubt from constant comparison or worried about what others will think? Why do you believe this occurs?

Are you ready to start boosting your self-esteem and rid yourself of self-doubt?

What is one thing you can do today to ditch self-doubt? Are you ready?

CHAPTER 3

Marriage

I've always looked at marriage as two imperfect people unwilling to give up on each other. A bond created out of mutual respect, love, and admiration.

It's amazing, exciting, scary, intense, happy, sad, and hilarious all at the same time. It's the one hardest relationship in life and yet the most fulfilling.

Whether you are planning to get hitched or are already in a marriage, I hope the following stories about marriage provide you with some insight into and understanding about your own relationship.

> "Love is giving someone the power to destroy you,
> but trusting them not to."
> ~ Unknown

You Had Me at Harry

I'm going to marry this man, I thought as I opened my gift. It was a present I'd never expected. A gift of immeasurable value and an unspoken significance that meant more to me than he would ever know.

You see, almost a year before, I was in the midst of a terrible divorce. Days were filled with arguments over finances, custody of our son, and how to split up our possessions. It was exhausting, frustrating, and heartbreaking.

Surprisingly, we did agree on one thing: who would take which vehicle. We mutually decided I would keep the SUV and he would take the car. It was an unexpected pleasant relief to have a civil conversation.

What I didn't realize when my ex drove off that day was the CD organizer we both shared was in his car. Long before the days of iTunes and smart phone playlists, the car CD holder was a music lover's treasured library. Ours was a master collection of carefully curated and catalogued music to reflect both our tastes. My ex filled it with alternative favourites, whereas I lined the case with pop icons and my entire collection of Harry Connick Jr. CDs.

It wasn't until I was reaching for the CD holder the next day that I realized he had it. I called him immediately.

"What CDs?" was his response.

"My Harry Connick Jr. CDs. I'm not too bothered about the other discs, but I would really appreciate it if you could return the jazz CDs," I answered, a little confused by his response.

"Sorry, I don't know what you're talking about. I have the case, but I don't have your CDs," he refuted.

"Are you kidding me? I know for a fact those CDs are in the case," I contended.

"Nope! I don't have your CDs. You're mistaken."

"I don't want to fight about this, but you know I've been collecting the Harry CDs for a long time. Can you please look again?" I begged.

"I've just looked and none of your CDs are in the case."

"This is silly, you know they're in there. What would be the point of keeping them from me when you don't even like the music?" I questioned.

"I don't know what to tell you. I don't have your CDs!" He hung up the phone.

I couldn't believe it. I was absolutely dumbfounded by his reaction. Why would he lie?

For days I agonized over the conversation and wanted to call and demand he return them. Yet in the end, I decided to let it go. Sometimes you just need to pick your battles, and I felt this was one I didn't want to have and probably wouldn't win.

Months later there was still no respite from the ongoing battle with my ex. I'd actually found I was becoming quite numb to it. It also helped that I'd recently become distracted by a new love interest, or should I say comrade.

His name was Mike, and just like me, he was in the middle of a messy divorce.

Quickly we became each other's confidants. It was nice to be with someone who understood and tolerated what I was going through. We even joked that our relationship worked because we both knew it was much cheaper than therapy. In fact, many evenings were spent bitching and bonding about our exes. Chatting over a pizza one night, I decided to dramatically share the Harry Connick Jr. CD story.

Mike laughed at my silly impersonation of my ex and asked, "Did you ever get your CDs back?"

"Nope. He's probably listening to them and sipping brandy in his evil lair as we speak," I answered, giggling at my shameful comment.

Mike chuckled. "You're ridiculous."

"Yep, just another day on the battleground . . . right?" I laughed.

Yet for some reason, lying in bed that night I didn't seem to find the story so funny. In fact, reminiscing about this particular argument seemed to trigger and unearth some pretty painful emotions I hadn't even realized I hadn't dealt with.

I cried for hours that night.

Left feeling heartbroken from the experience, I could also feel myself becoming much more guarded around Mike in the days that followed. I was intentionally hiding any vulnerability as a means to protect myself from feeling pain like that again. All I kept thinking was, if a person who had loved me could wound me so easily, how could I trust someone who barely knew me?

Mike immediately noticed my distance and tried several times to broach the subject. I continually brushed him off. Keeping my heart safe was my only priority. If he didn't like it and decided to leave, it was probably for the best.

Gratefully, Mike never left.

Weeks turned into months, and before I knew it we were celebrating Christmas and Mike had handed me a wrapped box to open.

"Oh my God, what did you do?" I asked, completely surprised as I opened the package.

"I didn't know which Harry Connick Jr. CDs you owned, so I just bought every title I could find. I know you had joked when you told me the story, but I feel they really meant something to you, and I wanted to make sure you had your collection back," he explained.

I just sat there in disbelief and stared at the CDs. Tears started rolling down my cheeks.

Mike grabbed my hands. "Are you upset with me?" he asked.

"No, I'm not upset. I love you and I love this thoughtful gift more than you will ever know. I just can't believe you remembered after all these months," I confessed, as I reached out and kissed him.

It truly felt like a Christmas miracle. The CDs had initially been the catalyst to shutting my heart away, and yet now they were the reason my heart was opening up again.

What I've learned is when it comes to trusting each other, we need to accept that our past is not our present. We need to be able to recognize that what hurt us before is not necessarily what is currently standing before us—even when the situation looks frighteningly similar.

Mike taught me that trust and love were possible again with his incredible gift, a gesture that made me realize I wanted to spend the rest of my life with him. And a year and half later we made it official. We've now been married for fourteen amazing years.

Does this mean I won't ever get hurt again or people won't let me down? Nope. That's the game of life. Yet if I never allow myself to be vulnerable, I will never make the incredible connections I deserve or create a new reality—one where I learn that the only way to know if I can trust somebody is to trust them.

I hope you're able to do the same.

Questions: You Had Me at Harry

Do you struggle with trust?

Did the story help you recall your own heartbreak from the past? Are you still carrying the pain, or have you been able to forgive and open your heart again to trust?

If not, why?

How does not being able to trust make you feel?

Do you find it hard to let anyone in until they've earned it ten times over?

Do you find yourself questioning if you will ever trust anyone again? Why do you feel that is?

Would you like to start trusting again?

How do you feel you could begin trusting again? Name one thing you could do differently.

"What counts in making a happy marriage is not so much how compatible you are, but how you deal with incompatibility."
~ Leo Tolstoy

Marriage Is a Rainbow

I recently met up with two friends I hadn't seen in ages. We clinked glasses and agreed it had been way too long since we'd done this.

When a reunion happens with friends I haven't seen in a while, one thing I always wonder is why, after so many failed attempts to make it happen, had we chosen this particular evening to get together? In some cases, it's days or weeks before I figure it out. But tonight, the question was answered for me immediately.

A moment after we took our first sip, my girlfriend took a deep breath and blurted that her husband had left her the night before. She called it a trial separation. I gasped and reached out my hand to console her. This was a huge surprise, and not the good kind.

For the rest of the evening, we listened intently to what had happened. She told us about all the good years, and the terrible months that had followed them. Though I was grateful she felt comfortable enough to share this with us, my heart was breaking for her.

As she recounted the last few weeks, I thought about how truly amazing it is when two people decide to spend their lives together. It's beautiful, colourful, and downright magical. But it can also be difficult, frustrating, and painful. Sometimes it feels like a miracle that any relationship survives.

I desperately wanted to offer my friend some advice or insight, anything to give her hope. So I decided to share a special message I'd created and written about marriage for a friend's wedding I'd officiated.

"A marriage is a rainbow," I told her.

"When a couple first meet, the purple hue of the rainbow appears—the first colour band of their relationship. This shade is fun, dreamlike, and truly passionate.

"With every touch you feel butterflies and fireworks. Your mind is filled with thoughts of them and nothing but them. It's pure chemistry!"

My friend smiled like she was remembering those days fondly.

"But a rainbow has many colours," I continued. As the relationship buds and then blooms, passionate purple welcomes a glorious shade of red.

"Love!"

"Or anger," she observed, giggling. That was definitely true.

I smiled and continued with my explanation.

"Love hits you like a ton of bricks. It knocks the air out of your lungs, leaves you reeling, and is the best feeling in the world. It's euphoric. Lust turns into trust, and commitment just feels right."

Her eyes started to water. "He said 'I love you' first," she said, her voice cracking.

I let her hold onto that moment for a minute and then I resumed.

"A ceremony happens and the orange colour band is added. The blissful first year of marriage. It's delightful and sweet. Your rainbow is growing.

"You have a ring on your finger, a smile on your face, and wedding photos to prove your love for each other.

"Sexy lingerie, weekends full of fun, and dreams of an incredible future together. You truly believe you're winning at marriage, and life is amazing!"

"Such an amazing year," she interjected. "We were broke, but incredibly in love."

We all smiled.

"Eventually the soft hue of yellow is added," I went on.

"This colour feels like a hug, or a warm blanket on a cold day. It's also track pants, no makeup, and weekends on the couch with Netflix and Doritos. It's warm, comfortable contentment.

"Yellow in any marriage is blissful, but this shade comes with a warning. Comfort can easily turn into boredom if the passion of purple and the fun of orange are forgotten."

"Isn't that the truth," she said, and we all laughed.

"Then, without warning, blue appears. This tint is life. Reality crashing the party.

"A parent dies. Someone loses their job. It's depression, stress, ego, and arguments. The blues. This particular band of colour can easily shake any relationship to its core.

"When added to a tightly woven rainbow, some couples sail through, their relationship stronger than ever. Other couples fall apart; their rainbow fades from the sky."

A tear rolled down my friend's cheek.

I reached out for her hand and said, "But hovering at the end of this wondrous spectrum is a beautiful shade of green.

"Forgiveness, empathy, compassion, and kindness. These things are crucial for any relationship to survive through tough times like these. Green is a fresh start.

"When we gaze at a rainbow in the sky, an individual colour doesn't occur alone. All are present and beautiful, existing as one. For a marriage to flourish, each hue must be experienced, embraced, and endured."

As I finished my story, I looked into my friend's teary eyes and said, "Your rainbow may be hidden behind some storm clouds at the moment. But eventually the rain will stop and the sun will appear.

"As this happens, my hope for the two of you is that you realize your magnificent, glorious rainbow can shine brightly once again. Please don't forget all the years and all the colours that went into creating your marriage."

Most of all, remember that a rainbow always shines brightest after a storm.

Questions: Marriage Is a Rainbow

Can you remember adding each rainbow colour to your relationship? Feeling the passion of purple, the red love, the comfortable yellow, and so on?

What rainbow colour do you feel you are in now?

What rainbow relationship colour has been your favourite and why?

What rainbow colour would you rather be in your relationship and why? How do you feel you could reach or get back to that colour?

"For every minute you remain angry, you give up
sixty seconds of peace of mind."
~ Ralph Waldo Emerson

The "Right" Bench

Have you ever been blood-curdling, foaming-at-the-mouth
angry, so angry that you see red?

It happens. We all have our breaking points. A car cutting
us off. Someone disrespecting us or talking back, or maybe it's
plans being cancelled last minute. Whatever the hot button is,
it's an adrenalin-pumping fury that can cause you to explode. It
happens to the best of us.

In my case, I don't often get very angry. In fact, it's pretty rare.
Yet in the past, this wasn't always the case. I actually seemed to
have an insufferable need to always be right. At least that was
until the day I threatened my husband with murder.

The offence actually took place a number of years ago when
Mike and I decided to redecorate the front sunroom in our house.
We gave the walls a fresh coat of white paint, bought a new rug,
and hung some framed flower photos I'd taken in my backyard.
While out shopping, we also found a red wooden bench. We both
agreed it was the finishing touch, and Mike said he'd assemble it
when we arrived home.

When we pulled in the driveway, I carried a couple of grocery
bags into the house and Mike grabbed the bench. Yet for some

reason Mike didn't leave the box in the sunroom. He walked through the empty, newly decorated room and through the living room before dropping it in the dining area and heading to the basement to grab his tools.

Noticing this, I hollered downstairs, asking why he had left the bench box in the dining room.

"To put together," he yelled up.

I shook my head. "That doesn't make any sense."

"What? Give me a minute, I'll be right up."

Less than a minute later Mike was back upstairs with a couple of screwdrivers. He grabbed himself a beer and asked, "Now what were you yelling about?"

"The bench," I said, standing over it with my hands on my hips. "Why are you putting it together in the dining room?"

"Why not?" he asked, baffled by my line of questioning.

"That makes absolutely no sense," I protested. "Why wouldn't you put it together in the empty sunroom where it belongs?"

"Because I just want to put it together here," he casually answered and proceeded to open the box.

"Yes, but if you put it together here, then we'll have to carry it through the WHOLE house back into the sunroom. This makes no sense and is completely illogical."

He continued opening the box. "What does it matter?"

"It matters because this is not logical thinking," I answered, feeling a little frustrated by his nonchalant attitude.

"I'm putting it together here," he strongly stated as he continued what he was doing.

"Fine," I huffed. "But you need to admit that putting it together here ISN'T logical thinking."

"Heidi, I don't need to admit anything, because it doesn't matter."

"It does matter!" I then proceeded to enlighten him again with a complete reiteration that the bench doesn't belong in the dining room, but it belongs in the sunroom. I followed up with just how much space exists in there to put it together. I finished my argument with just how easy it would be to move it into its place, instead of carrying it through the entire house.

Mike didn't seem to be impressed with my argument. He just shot me a disparaging look. When you've been married as long as we have, you understand that "that look" means he was done listening to me.

Frustrated with him, I stomped off into the kitchen to put the groceries away. However, in my mind this wasn't over yet.

From the kitchen pass-through I could see the bench parts scattered throughout the dining room. It made my blood boil, and I just couldn't let it go.

"Once it's together it's going to be awkward carrying it into the sunroom," I chirped from the kitchen.

"I'm not worried."

"Yes, but I am!" I hollered. "Why can't you just agree that the bench should be put together in the sunroom?"

"Because it really doesn't matter where it's put together. The only thing that's important is it WILL be put together."

His indifference infuriated me.

"Mike I'm really, really mad at you right now," I pronounced, walking back into the dining room.

"Heidi, you're acting ridiculous."

"I don't think you understand. I feel like I could cry in anger right now. You need to admit that what you're doing is illogical," I shrieked, standing over him with my hands frantically waving in the air.

He just silently stared at me, sipping his beer.

"Nothing?" I asked, absolutely fuming.

It was at this point that all rational thinking disappeared and my inner Hulk ego awoke, ready to destroy.

Seething red, my heart racing and fists in the air, I frantically screamed, "I'm so furious I could grab a knife and stab you right now!"

I definitely got his attention at this point because Mike stopped what he was doing, stood up, took another sip of his beer, and sarcastically remarked, "Really? Who's being logical now?"

Shocked, I gasped.

"Right?" Mike asked.

Oh my God, he's right, I thought and burst out laughing.

Eckhart Tolle once described the need to be right as a form of ridiculous violence. I had definitely tested and proven that theory.

Thank God for Mike's quick wit and sarcasm. Without it I may have spent the rest of my days in an orange jumpsuit.

All kidding aside, I never would have harmed my husband, but I was pretty shocked to realize how incredibly attached I was to being right. Nobody likes to be on the losing end of an argument—but I needed to ask myself what was more important: being right or being compassionate.

When we make an effort to prove someone wrong by establishing ourselves as right, we're being heartless in the process, whether we intend to or not. I realize we all struggle with the insecurities of our egos, but we should never let our egos be the winners in life.

Of course, I'm not saying I need to agree with everyone. It's about giving up the need to always be right, leaving my ego behind. Especially when the price you pay for it is being hurtful, impatient, and insensitive, or in my case a complete lunatic.

Dr. Wayne Dyer famously wrote, "When given the choice between being right and being kind, choose kind." And that's exactly what I plan on doing from now on!

Questions: The "Right" Bench

Could you see yourself in my story? Do you struggle with the need to be right all the time?

What was the last thing you needed to be right about?

Why do you feel it's important to always be right?

How does it make you feel to always fight to be right?

Would you rather be right or happy? Explain why?

Are you ready in life to let go of being right?

> "We must accept finite disappointment,
> but never lose infinite hope."
> ~ Martin Luther King Jr.

What a Difference Twenty-Four Hours Makes

My phone buzzed, and I almost knocked it off my desk in my eagerness to grab it. I looked at the screen, and my shoulders slumped. I barely saw what it was but knew it wasn't what I was waiting for. Again. I let out the breath I was holding.

How many times could a person feel this way, excited then deflated, again and again in an endless loop? It was agonizing. The wait continued. My phone lay motionless next to my mousepad. I willed myself to stop staring at it and get back to work. So of course that's when it buzzed again. I snatched it.

It was an email from my boss. Can you come to my office? *Oh my goodness. Could this be it?* A surge of adrenalin started pumping through me.

"Be there in 5," I typed back.

I could barely breathe as I walked to her office. It couldn't be healthy for my heart to beat this fast. The only thought that calmed me was that, for better or worse, I'd finally have my answer. The suspense would be over at last.

My boss sat me down and got right to the point.

"I'm sorry, Heidi, but we've decided to go with someone else."

The world stopped.

"Not that you couldn't do the job. It came down to experience, and the other candidate had more," she explained.

I sank in my chair. My heart mimicked the motion in my chest. I hadn't realized just how much I'd wanted the new job until I didn't get it. It was like a physical blow. It was like that feeling when the home team almost wins a really close game. Multiplied by a thousand or so. The crowd sighs.

I replayed the job interview over and over in my head. I thought I'd nailed it. It couldn't have just been a matter of experience, right? I wasn't letting myself off the hook that easy. Really, where did I go wrong?

I wanted the ground to open up and swallow me whole. Was that too much to ask for? I hated this feeling I was experiencing. Disappointment. Disappointment that I didn't get the job, and disappointment in myself. I hadn't felt this let down in a really long time. Six years or so, actually.

In 2005, my husband and I invested everything we had and purchased a bridal gown boutique. The timing was perfect. Some friends of ours wanted to retire early, and they were thrilled we were willing to buy it. They even held the mortgage for us to take it over. We were very grateful.

The first few years were amazing! Business was good, and days working in the boutique were filled with laughter, tears of joy, and beautiful family moments. I loved it.

But by the end of the third year, my sparkly dream started to tarnish. The country was heading into a recession, and we quickly started to feel the strain. Our accountants explained that wedding gowns were considered a luxury item, and that in times of recession, they're usually the first thing people start cutting back on. They recommended we sell or close the shop before things got too out of control.

No way. Wedding gowns are too important to a bride, I thought. Turns out I was wrong. As predicted by the professionals, the year that followed was difficult. But I didn't want to give it up yet. We weathered the storm.

And as we headed into our fifth year, things actually started to turn around. The brides were back in full force, and so were their wedding dress budgets. Sales were increasing, and the financial storm clouds were clearing. We'd fought with everything we had—and it looked like it was starting to pay off.

Then, out of nowhere, we were blindsided. The original owners of the boutique suddenly wanted their mortgage to be paid in full. We were nervous that we might not be able to secure such a large loan with the bank.

We talked to every financial institute, credit union, and mortgage broker who would meet with us, but rejection followed us everywhere we went. We felt like we were living a nightmare. With no other option, we decided to come to settlement with the original owners. We would take a substantial loss, and they would become the owners of the business and building again.

After all the ups and downs we'd been through, the battle was over and we had lost. We were emotionally and financially devastated by this turn of events. We had lost so much: our livelihood, our identity, our friends.

It was heartbreaking. I cried for weeks. Then one evening before bed, Mike seemed to realize I needed to feel hope again and said something to me that changed everything.

"What a difference twenty-four hours will make. Just believe it and it will happen," he spoke.

They were simple words, but I was desperate to feel better. So I held onto the words and hoped maybe I would feel better the next day.

The next evening, we both agreed it had surprisingly helped. For the next few months we both repeated the same hopeful mantra every night before bed: what a difference twenty-four hours will make.

It worked. I really began to believe that every day I'd feel a little better than the last. And I did. With our new-found attitude, things slowly got better, and our finances began to improve.

Eventually, I found an amazing new job working in television, and the sting of disappointment was long forgotten. At one time, it had seemed like my whole world was imploding, but now I barely thought about those times. Funny how you can get over things.

Sitting at work now, still reeling from the bad news, I pondered my latest upset and felt my mood lighten just a little bit. I didn't get the new job, and sure that was upsetting, but it wasn't the end of the world. *Give it twenty-four,* I thought.

Time eases pain, gives perspective, and allows us an opportunity to plan our next move. Because there will be a next move. So whether you're down about a job, a crush, or any other disappointment life throws at you, just remember that you'll feel better with every passing day. I did. Give it twenty-four.

Questions: What a Difference Twenty-Four Hours Makes

Can you remember a time when the sting of disappointment crippled you? What happened?

How did you deal with the disappointment, or are you still dealing with it?

When disappointment occurs, are you someone who spends time ruminating over the injustices that have happened, constantly asking yourself how, why, and why me? Be honest with yourself.

Why do you feel it's hard to let go of disappointment?

How do you generally deal with disappointment?

Do you believe, you can actually feel better after twenty-four hours and then implement the practice again and again until you feel better?

If not, what do you think is stopping you?

"You are what you do, not what you say you'll do."
~ Carl Gustav Jung

The Big Talk

Remember talking the big game and showing off your skills when you were a kid? Anything from bragging how fast you could run or how high you could climb to being able to eat the most pizza slices in one sitting. This invincible, fearless attitude helped us achieve anything we wanted.

Actually, blowing our own horn was motivating us to achieve our hopes and dreams, teaching us to be passionate, to take action and live a life of fulfillment and meaning. Yet somehow as we grew older, many of us lost our unconquerable boldness. We still love to talk the big talk, but we've let our comfort zones and fear prevent us from following through.

There are so many familiar big talks. I'm going to lose ten pounds. My biggest dream is to write a book. I'm quitting this job for something better. Yet years later the ten pounds hasn't been lost, there was always an excuse why the book wasn't started, and lo and behold, a better job never came along.

We've all done it. In fact, it's actually something I witnessed almost every time my husband and his best friend got together. Both were successful, hard-working men, with very comfortable lives and a love for the "big talk." Especially when both had had a few beers when our families got together at his friend's cottage every summer.

Every cabin conversation was pretty much the same. They were either planning to build something incredible, organizing an epic boys' trip, or designing a mind-blowing invention. Yet their plans were no more than legendary myths, never to be achieved.

That was, until one summer when I just couldn't hold my tongue any longer. The cottage weekend started out just like every other year. A new plan was hatched and the big boastful talk had begun. This year's ambitious plan included buying motorcycles and taking an epic road trip across the country. Their insane destination? Tijuana, Mexico. They even compared themselves to James Dean in *Rebel Without a Cause.*

Now I've heard everything, I thought. Neither of them rode or had motorcycle licences, not to mention I'd never even heard either of them say they had any interest in bikes. This plan was starting to sound more like *"Rebel Without a Clue."*

Sitting in the hot tub after dinner, my girlfriend and I noticed the men were really starting to get creative with their motorcycle delusion. They spoke about building custom bikes, growing handlebar moustaches, purchasing leather chaps, and creating a gang name. I had to admit this year's plan was by far the coolest one yet. I was a little disappointed it would never come to fruition.

The next night the four of us found ourselves back in the hot tub, both men goading each other to come up with bigger badass plans for their motorcycle fantasy.

I don't know if it was my disappointment, my tolerance level, or maybe a little liquid courage, but out of nowhere I blurted, "You guys don't have the BALLS to make this happen!"

My girlfriend gasped.

Both men puffed up their chests, clearly offended their manhood was on the line, and simultaneously responded, "WHAAAAAAAAAAAT?"

Not being someone who backs down to a little opposition, I repeated myself. "I think you heard me . . . you guys don't have the balls to make this happen."

"Wanna make a bet?" my husband responded in his deepest and most masculine tone.

"Yeah! I'll gladly take that bet," I quickly responded, not believing my luck. Their lack of following through was a guaranteed win for me.

The bet we agreed on gave them two years to purchase motorcycles, learn to ride them, and then drive to San Diego, California, and back. We all decided it was best to eliminate another border by not going to Mexico.

If they won, I owed them one hundred dollars each. If I won, or should I say, when, they were to purchase me a pair of Christian Louboutin shoes of my choice. After the official handshake, I couldn't help but picture the famous red-bottomed stilettos already on my feet. *Too bad I'll have to wait two years to get them*, I thought.

Unfortunately, I never received those beautiful pumps.

Shockingly, the following spring, both men passed their motorcycle tests and then purchased new bikes. Yet even more astonishing, they actually set off on their adventurous road trip with three other bikers and a chase vehicle just before their deadline was up. Their GPS was set for San Diego, California. They even called themselves the "No Balls to Blue Balls" crew.

It's always fun to talk and plan about big dreams. There's nothing wrong with having a little fun. But without any action or follow-through, your dreams can only be called wishes—

blowing in the wind, never to be fulfilled, achieved, or experienced.

I realize chasing after your dreams can be scary, but what's the worst thing that could happen? In most cases you'll probably end up feeling happier and healthier while having a whole lot more fun in life. Not to mention, you made your dreams come true.

For both men, it's not that they were never doers in life, but it had become clear they had gotten used to living in their comfort zones—daring to talk the big talk but forgetting to live it. Yet life isn't just about surviving, it's about truly living.

It's been a number of years since the legendary bet, and I'm grateful to say their traditional "big-plan cottage talks" revolve only around motorcycle adventures—and they do take. They've realized doing is a lot more fun than just planning.

So whether you're talking about your next dream career, a new home, your soulmate, or a new interest, stop talking and start betting on your own life. Believe me, you will always end up a winner.

Questions: The Big Talk

Do you love to talk the "big talk"? Always talking about what you're going to do instead of doing it?

What do you feel is preventing you from pulling the trigger on your dreams? Is it fear, money, family, or too many excuses? Be honest with yourself.

If nothing was standing in your way, what dream would you love to achieve? Would you travel, start your own business, go back to school, or chase your dream job?

On a scale of 1 to 10 (10 being the greatest), how much would you love to make your dream come true? Really admit to yourself how important it is.

What is one small thing you can do today to start moving towards your dream? Warning: You may have automatically just come up with several excuses. Do your best to put them aside and truthfully answer the question.

If you answered the last question, be proud of yourself. Now list the second thing you could do to make your dream come true, and once you have done that, list the third thing. I realize this is probably scary and your brain is racing with a million excuses, but you can do this because your life is the most important life and you deserve to make your dreams come true.

Once you have listed three things you can do to start moving towards your dream, set yourself a deadline. This part is hard but incredibly necessary to enlist your subconscious to help you achieve your dream. You can do this! I believe in you!

Congratulations! You are now a doer and not just a "big talker" anymore!

CHAPTER 4

Kids

As a parent, it's our job to teach our kids everything. It starts with walking, talking, and potty training, followed by manners, rules, and values to function in this amazing world.

Throughout each and every stage, I've been grateful to help mould my kids into the incredible human beings they've become—shaping their lives by my actions, advice, insight, and wisdom.

However, I've come to realize I wasn't the only one dispensing knowledge. In fact, they were actually teaching me as well. In this chapter I dive into some pretty astounding lessons I learned through my kids. All are wonderful moments that taught me to embrace love, joy, and understanding to the fullest.

"I stopped trying to be perfect when I realized
it's enough to be present."
~ Curtis Tyrone Jones

The Video Game of Life

G rowing up, it was always implied to me that profound wisdom and knowledge came from people older and wiser
than I was—folks like my parents, grandparents, doctors, and
even teachers. Yes, there would be smaller life lessons resulting
from experiences, but the most important insight would be from
the latter.

Yet what I've actually come to realize is this isn't always the
case. In fact, some of my most powerful life lessons have all
come from what I like to call "the game of life." Unexpected
life events, experiences, setbacks, mistakes, and even unlikely
people of all ages and professions.

However, the most unforgettable education I ever received
was from my son when he was only five years old.

"Michael, it's 8:00 p.m., time to put your Game Boy away
and get ready for bed," I affectionately said, stroking his hair.

"Five more minutes. I really want to show you all my new
Pokémon guys. PLEEEEASE," he begged.

Michael had gotten a Game Boy for his birthday and was
immediately obsessed with it. I on the other hand had no
interest in it and hoped the video game phase would be short

lived. Especially since it was becoming an issue every night before bed.

"Not tonight," I answered, holding my hand out for him to pass me the game device.

"Fine! You never want to see my game," he exclaimed, handing it to me with utter disdain.

"Michael, that's enough. It's just a game." I proceeded to lecture him on the bedtime rules.

Two stories later, all teddy bears and a sleepy little boy tucked in, I closed his bedroom door and headed to the family room for a quiet night in front of the TV. At the time I lived in a raised bungalow, which meant the living room, kitchen, and bedrooms were all on the same floor and the family room was downstairs. Now with my feet up and a glass of wine in hand, I started channel surfing. Ten minutes later, I was already starting to nod off when I heard what sounded like little feet walking around upstairs.

Maybe he had to go to the bathroom, I thought and headed up to investigate.

I quickly checked the bathroom and kitchen. No Michael. I checked his room. No Michael. Then as I walked back down the hallway, towards the living room, a low muffled noise from behind my bedroom door stopped me in my tracks. Slowly opening the door, I found Michael—lying on my bed with his hands behind his head, casually watching TV.

"Hey, hey, what's going on here?" I asked, with an accusatory tone.

Michael sat up immediately with a guilty look on his face. "Nothing."

"Michael James, you know the bedtime rule is 8:00 p.m. with no exceptions. Now get back to bed," I sternly demanded.

Realizing the jig was up, Michael quickly jumped up and ran back to his room and hopped into bed. Following him, I firmly informed him that since he broke the rules, his bedtime would be fifteen minutes earlier the next night. The punishment seemed to work because I didn't hear a peep from him for the rest of the night.

The following evening, I stuck to the punishment and started Michael's bedtime routine fifteen minutes earlier, but not without some flak.

"Aww, Mommy, I don't wanna go to bed so early. You still haven't let me show you my new game," he whined.

"Enough with the game, Michael. Please put it away and get ready for bed. You broke the rules and now you have to pay the consequences," I strongly stated.

To show me he wasn't impressed, he disappointingly turned and walked off doing his best impersonation of what I would call "dead man walking" towards his room. He'd always been one for the dramatics, but tonight was Oscar-worthy. I actually chuckled inside but kept a poker-straight face to show him I was serious.

Once Michael's bedtime routine was complete and he was all tucked in, I reminded him not to get up again and warned him there would be harsher consequences if he did. Michael agreed he wouldn't get up. I believed him. I kissed him goodnight and headed downstairs.

Five minutes later I couldn't believe my ears when I heard Michael running around upstairs.

"Are you kidding me?" I mouthed to myself as I stomped up the stairs.

"Michael, what are you doing up again!" I snapped when I found him in my bed again watching TV.

Startled, Michael jumped up and scurried past me without a word, like a little mouse escaping his capture. I angrily followed him, declaring his new bedtime was thirty minutes earlier the next night. I also threatened the earlier bedtime for a week if he got up again that evening. He must have realized how serious I was because I didn't hear a peep from the little mouse for the rest of the night.

By the third night I was determined to kick Michael's unacceptable sneaky habit. At 7:30 p.m. on the dot, I demanded Michael's Game Boy and ushered him off to bed with a heavy-handed warning of an hour earlier bedtime punishment if he defiantly got up again. Feeling satisfied I'd gotten my point across, I kissed him goodnight and went downstairs.

"For the love of God!" I frustratingly said out loud. It had been only three minutes since I'd put Michael to bed and he was up again.

"That little bugger." I could feel my blood boil as I ran up the stairs.

"Michael James, I've just about had it with you! What are you doing up again?" I screamed as I entered my room, completely at my wits' end. "I warned you about your new punishment! Do you honestly want to go to bed an hour earlier?"

"No, Mommy," he answered.

"Then why do you keep getting up?"

"Because I don't care about the punishment," he boldly answered.

"Excuse me?" I exclaimed in complete disbelief of his cheek.

Then Michael climbed off the bed and stood directly in front of me and confidently told me, "Mommy, you keep punishing me with something that doesn't matter to me. If you punished me with something that I actually cared about, I promise I won't get up anymore."

In complete astonishment by his answer, but very curious what he thought was a better punishment, I demanded he tell me how he thought I should punish him.

With his hands on his hips he proceeded to tell me. "Well, Mommy, I really love my Game Boy, and if you told me I couldn't play it for a day, I would never break the rules and get up again."

I just stood there.

To say I was awe-struck by his answer would be an understatement. I was honestly stunned and absolutely speechless.

"Mommy, what do you think?" Michael asked, breaking me out of my dazed trance.

"Right. Tomorrow you are banned from using your Game Boy for the entire day," I pronounced like I had something to do with this brilliant punishment.

"Great. Now I won't get up anymore," he answered and scurried off to bed.

Again, I just stood there in complete shock. I was absolutely dumbfounded by my son's insightful awareness, wisdom, and confidence. I even questioned who was parenting who in the moment.

What I finally came to realize when the astonishment wore off was that Michael had been trying to show me what was important in his life for days. Yet I'd been so focused on the significance of routines and rules that I'd not been paying attention to what was meaningful to Michael—his Game Boy.

Michael helped me understand that as humans we all want to be acknowledged, appreciated, seen, and heard. Yet when this doesn't occur we instinctually act out physically or verbally. For some this shows up as disobeying rules, losing your temper, disengaging from people, or turning to coping mechanisms like food or alcohol. However, when we are able to put aside our own agendas and truly listen to each other, we feel accepted, understood, valued, and validated.

The next morning after breakfast I placed Michael's Game Boy in front of him and asked him to show me his new Pokémon characters. Completely surprised yet unsure if this was a test, he reminded me he was grounded from his game for the day.

I was impressed and proud of his honesty, but I explained I'd decided to forgo his punishment as long as he promised not to get up anymore and then showed me his game. He enthusiastically agreed he wouldn't get up and gave me a giant hug.

For the next thirty minutes I sat and I listened and watched in amazement as he passionately explained each and every little creature's information. His knowledge of the game was like a professional sportscaster announcing the stats of a draft pick. It was impressive.

To date it's one of my fondest memories.

Michael stuck to his promise that night, and because of that I also pledged to always listen, support, and acknowledge what he was passionate about, even if I didn't understand it.

Michael's love for video games continued throughout his childhood and into his adulthood, and I always did my best to keep up and listen. This fascination also continued when Michael enrolled in college as a video game program developer and then eventually graduated with honours. I'm so proud of him.

So, no matter where, when, or from whom a lesson appears, it's up to us to listen and live and learn from the "game of life," or in my case, the "video game of life."

Questions: The Video Game of Life

Did the story remind you of a lesson you may have learned from an unlikely person or experience but didn't realize it at the time?

What was the lesson? How or from whom did you learn it?

Have there been moments in your life when you felt you weren't being heard or acknowledged? How did you react and how did it make you feel?

Do you realize your actions or reactions may have occurred because you weren't being acknowledged?

Did the story help you realize why other people may have reacted the way they did towards you in the past? Could there have been times when life got in the way of acknowledging someone? Be honest with yourself.

Awareness is the key and window to emotional intelligence. Did the story give you some awareness that there may be someone you can reach out to today to let them know why you acted or reacted the way you did in the past?

Is there someone you would like to contact and apologize to for not seeing and acknowledging them in the past?

"If you change the way you look at things,
the things you look at change."
~ Dr. Wayne Dyer

Everybody's Got a Story

Since launching the Positive People Army, I've been amazed by the huge outpouring of support I've received. Many people have reached out to share the most intimate details of their lives, good and bad. I've always felt that people had an ease and openness around me, but what's happening now is definitely out of the ordinary.

When I mentioned this increase in messages to my husband, Mike, he smiled and said it was because I was now relatable.

"Relatable? What do you mean by that? I have always been relatable."

"Heidi, you are very accomplished," he said. "Anything and everything you have ever set your mind to, you have done. Not to mention you're creative, opinionated, attractive, and very positive. For some people you could be very intimidating. Since launching the PPA, you've shared and admitted that you experience vulnerability, fear, and sadness. You're now relatable to people."

I was complimented, but they were hard words to hear. Making connections with people has always been one of the most important aspects of my life. I just couldn't imagine myself being intimidating or unapproachable. It was tough to digest. Did people honestly think I was intimidating? Did they really think I hadn't experienced heartache or failure?

For days I thought about his words. *You are now relatable.* One question kept occurring to me, over and over: Why do we have to admit our anxieties and doubts to be relatable?

Perception is a funny thing. You never really know who someone is until you've walked in their shoes. Yet without ever doing so, we quickly judge each other.

This made me think of when my son Michael was in grade three. We moved to another city, which meant a new school, new friends, new everything. He couldn't wait to meet his new classmates. When I dropped him off for his first day, he yanked off his seatbelt and leapt from the car, buzzing with excitement. He ran off into the school with fearless enthusiasm.

When I went to pick him up at the end of the day, I expected him to run towards me, beaming and bursting with stories of all the new friends he'd made. That wasn't the case. With his shoulders slumped and his head hung low, he walked towards the car, looking defeated and miserable.

I asked him how his day was. He responded angrily, "It was the WORST day of my life!"

No parent ever wants to hear those words. Your imagination tends to wander to the worst-case scenario. "Did your teacher do something? Did someone bully you? Did you get hurt?"

"No. I hated what happened at recess."

"What happened?"

"We all went out for recess and the kids asked me to play tag, and one kid told me 'time out' was anything green on the playground."

Michael told his new friends that making everything green the time out was stupid. There were too many things on the playground that were green, which made the game unfair. It was way too hard to tag anyone out. He actually told them they needed to change the rules. He was a very self-assured kid.

But to his shock, his suggestions didn't go over very well. A few of the boys told him they weren't changing the rules, and that if he didn't like them he didn't have to play. Michael didn't like that answer at all. In fact, he spent the rest of recess sitting alone, watching them play without him.

He finished telling the story, crossing his arms tightly and pushing out his bottom lip. To a kid in grade three, this truly is the worst day ever.

Though my heart was breaking for him, I also felt quite proud he'd been so frank with his new friends. I reached out to him. He uncrossed his arms and let me hold his hand.

"Michael, you began in junior kindergarten at your last school, right?"

"Yes," he mumbled.

"And since kindergarten, up until you left that school, did you always play tag the same way, with the same set of time-out rules?"

"Of course!" he snapped.

"Well, Michael, if someone new came to your old school you wouldn't want that person telling you how to play the game. This new school starts in junior kindergarten. These kids have probably been playing tag with the same rules since they started."

He looked at me intently, and I could see the little wheels turning in his head.

"Ohhhhhhh," he said. "It's not that they don't know the rules are wrong. They just don't know any better. I get it!"

And with that he proclaimed that he would play with them tomorrow, now that he had more perspective on the situation. I chuckled at his answer.

Michael's initial quick judgment had led him to dismiss his new friends without even trying to understand them. I remind myself of this story all the time. It doesn't matter how someone looks, or what they say, or if they're successful or not. I always take a moment to put myself in their shoes, to ponder what they've been through to get to that point.

Everyone feels pain, vulnerability, and fear. Just because someone seems strong or like they have everything together, it doesn't mean they aren't fighting their own battles. Like anyone, they need compassion and empathy.

I'm glad that people perceive me as a more relatable person now. I hope my story will get others to second-guess their snap judgments and perceptions of people. The more we open up and share, the more we can come together, making this world a little easier to navigate.

At the end of the day, we're all playing on the same playground, after all.

Questions: Everybody's Got a Story

Is there someone in your life, at this moment, that you have judged because of who you think they may be? Maybe someone's really successful and you feel they're unapproachable, or someone is quiet and standoffish and you feel they're snobby. Name that person and who you think they are.

Why do you feel this way about them? Is there something within yourself that is causing you to feel this way?

Have you ever tried to put yourself in their shoes?

Has someone ever judged you for being something you're not? How did that make you feel?

Why do you feel someone may have misjudged you?

How would you like people to know you?

"Family isn't whose blood you carry. It's who you love
and who loves you back."

~ Unknown

Family Day

I love Family Day. It's a holiday that occurs in some Canadian
provinces. It was created to give people a chance to spend
more time with those they cherish most, and that's exactly what
many of us do.

I plan something every year to celebrate it. It's become one of
my favourite days of the year, always a blissful time with my two
boys and my amazing husband, Mike. It also always reminds me
of the day I learned the true meaning of family.

Right after finishing university, I got married and enrolled in
a college to get some more hands-on education. While going to
school, I also worked in a group home for adults with mental and
physical disabilities.

It was there that I met Terry, a thirty-eight-year-old man
with Down syndrome. He had the mental capacity of someone
around five years old, and one of the biggest hearts of anyone
I've ever met.

Unlike many of the other residents, Terry hadn't grown up
in facility housing. He'd always lived with his mom and dad,
up until they passed away. I could see that the drastic change in
lifestyle was difficult for him to adjust to.

We quickly formed a bond. I'd look forward to seeing him every day. We'd often have coffee and doughnuts together or dance to club music in the living room, two of Terry's favourite activities. He was funny and caring, and he loved the Three Stooges. He was my friend.

Two years flew by. During the week of my college graduation, my first husband and I learned that we were expecting a baby. As the months passed and my delivery date grew closer, I felt both happy and sad. Though thrilled that I would soon be a mother, I knew that once I was on maternity leave, I wouldn't get to see Terry regularly anymore.

Then it hit me. I should just take Terry home to live with me. I know it sounds crazy, maybe just a result of all the pregnancy hormones. All I knew was it was the right decision. After countless conversations and a towering stack of paperwork, a stocky five-foot, forty-year-old Ukrainian man with Down syndrome moved into my house.

When Terry first moved in with me, his skills and vocabulary weren't the best. His parents had done pretty much everything for him, and even in the group home it had been largely the same.

I knew that with a baby on the way, I had to start teaching Terry more life skills. It was a slow process, but he was gradually catching on to the basics, day by day. I never felt frustrated, because it just felt right to have his beautiful energy in the house.

When Michael was born, Terry immediately fell in love with him and affectionately nicknamed him Bugaboo, a funny name that stuck for years. Michael's first year was wonderful, and Terry was right by his side for everything. To my surprise, Terry was absorbing everything I was teaching Michael.

As the years passed, Michael and Terry became inseparable. They were the very best of friends. And just as Michael's abilities increased, so did Terry's. They learned a lot from each other.

We never really discussed who Terry was in our lives, and Michael never thought to ask. Terry had just always been there, eternal and beloved. When strangers would ask Michael if he had any siblings, he would respond, "No, but I have a Terry!" It was cute.

Then one day, when we were out getting Michael's hair cut, something happened that forever changed the way I thought about family. While the stylist cut his hair, she asked him questions: Are you in school? What grade are you in? Do you like your teacher? He confidently answered all her questions with his adorable little voice.

And then she asked him if he had any brothers and sisters. Michael responded, "Yes, I do. I have a brother named Terry and he's forty-five years old!"

"Forty-five!" the hairstylist responded, confused. "Don't you mean four or five years old?"

"Nope, he's forty-five!"

I looked up from the magazine I was reading. I laughed, but as I thought about his answer, I realized the significance of what he'd just said.

On the drive home I asked Michael why he told the hairstylist that Terry was his brother. In a very matter-of-fact way, he said, "Because he is and I love him."

I was dumbfounded by his incredibly profound answer. I drove home speechless, tears rolling down my face. Without being taught or told, my five-year-old had figured out that we were a family. From that day forward, I introduced Terry as

Michael's brother. Some of the looks and questions I received over the years were hilarious.

Terry lived with us for over thirteen amazing years. In that time, I watched Michael quickly evolve into the role of big brother, even though Terry was forty years his senior. Michael read to him, protected him, cared for him, and watched him grow older. They were truly brothers.

Terry has since passed and we all miss him a lot, but what he brought to our family can never be replaced. He taught us that family doesn't just exist in the DNA. Family is a feeling. Family is love.

Since Terry left us, we continued growing our family unconventionally. Many of Michael's friends have lived in our house at times, and all of them are considered close family members. Though they've left the nest and moved on, they're still in our lives and still in our hearts.

For Family Day this year, I arranged for my family to celebrate at a new restaurant that had just opened. To my great surprise, as the afternoon progressed, all the friends who have called our house a home stopped by, one by one, to celebrate this day with us. As I sat there listening to everyone joke and share stories, I thought about Terry and the gift he brought our family.

I may only have a small family, technically speaking, but in reality, it's larger than life and still growing!

Questions: Family Day

What does family mean to you?

Do you believe family is more than just being related?

Who else do you consider family?

Why does this person feel more like family?

When was the last time you reached out to someone you feel is like family and let them know what they mean to you?

Celebrating family is celebrating love. What are you going to do to celebrate family?

"When you believe in yourself,
you have 100% of the people you need on your side."
~ Anima Vitam

Who's Living Your Life?

Something was wrong. I could tell from the moment she came
into the restaurant. It was in her eyes, in her smile, in her
walk. When you're good friends with someone you just have a
sixth sense for these things, no matter how long it's been since
you've seen them.

"We need to order a bottle of wine, pronto," she whispered in
my ear as we hugged.

I didn't need convincing, and after a few glasses of vino and
some well-needed catching up, my dear friend started to tell me
what was wrong.

Work had been terrible lately, she said. Actually, not just
lately. For years.

I could attest to that. I'd watched her go through it all. The
insane hours. The crushing workload. The, let's say, "difficult"
boss. But no matter how tough things got, my friend never
stopped fighting. She had a dream and she was going to make it
come true. Nothing and no one was going to stop her.

However, things had been especially bad lately. Her boss,
though a nightmare, was manageable. She could deal with that.
What she couldn't deal with was when a client told her he was

losing faith in her ability to complete a project, one she'd been slaving over for months.

That took its toll on her. It made her feel like she didn't have what it took after all. After everything she'd been through, maybe this was it. She felt like an Olympic runner tripping at the starting line, a failure before the race even began.

A tear ran down her face, then another. She took a breath, wiped her eyes, and appeared to compose herself. Then she began to weep. It made me want to cry along with her. All I wanted to do was help, but all I could do was take her hand.

I asked her if she was sure this is what she wanted to be doing. Did she even want that dream job promotion anymore?

She wiped her tears and looked like she was thinking it over. "Yes. But I don't know. Maybe they know better than me and I should just give up."

My heart sank for her. It's hard to see such a tough, effervescent lioness of a woman appear so defeated.

This all reminded me of something that happened with my youngest son, Haydn. Hoping to simultaneously distract and inspire her, I told her the story.

Haydn has always been extremely artistic. As a child, every notebook or scrap of paper had doodles or drawings on it. He loved to sketch, paint, and write the most elaborate short stories. When he entered grade 8, he had to choose his high school for the next year. Of course, Haydn wanted to go to an art school. In order to apply, he needed to submit a portfolio of his work, a letter of recommendation from his art teacher, and numerous referrals from people in the art community.

Our first step was meeting with his art teacher. When we walked into his classroom, I couldn't help but notice the walls were lined with artwork. I nudged Haydn and asked if some of the pieces were his. He grinned and said yes. Five of them.

The teacher and I sat down, and after exchanging some vapid pleasantries she asked Haydn what high school he wanted to apply to. Haydn excitedly answered that he wanted to go to Rosedale Heights School of the Arts.

"Well that's an ambitious thought," she quipped.

That didn't sit right with me. What was she implying?

"I'm sorry. Can you explain what you mean by that?"

"You need to understand that hundreds of kids apply every year, and Rosedale only accepts the MOST talented individuals." Oh, the way she said it. The most condescending tone you can imagine.

"Haydn is very talented."

"You're his mom. Of course, you would think that."

I was shocked and appalled by her answer! I looked at Haydn, and just like my girlfriend in the present-day restaurant, he looked defeated and miserable. In this moment my mama bear instincts were kicking in. How dare she say my son isn't talented?! I wanted to leap over the desk, rip her face off, and hang it up on the wall next to all the other art. I would call this piece *Justice*.

Somehow, I resisted. After all, I didn't want to see my son's future art through the glass partition of a prison visiting room. So I took a deep breath, tried to compose myself, and calmly asked her to point out some of Haydn's artwork on the walls and to explain why she thought my son wasn't talented enough.

She stared at me for a second, scoffed, and then scanned the walls looking for his work. After about a minute she crossed her arms and said she didn't know which art was his. It was very difficult for her to know each and every student's creation, she explained.

I looked at her in disbelief. I couldn't believe her audacity. She'd been so certain that Haydn wasn't art school material, and yet she had no idea what his art even looked like. I turned to Haydn and asked him to tell her which pieces were his. He pointed out five paintings hung throughout the classroom. They were brilliant.

To my surprise, she actually came down off her high horse and agreed that three of them were quite amazing. *Good thing I let her keep her face,* I thought.

Haydn was grinning from ear to ear.

So I slid the recommendation form over to her and politely asked her to reconsider her first response. She signed the form, and Haydn applied to the art school he wanted. Six weeks later he received a letter from them. He'd gotten in, of course, just like I knew he would. I used this experience to teach Haydn that he should never let another person's opinion dictate his life choices.

If you believe in something and you love it, then just do it. Don't ever listen to the naysayers; don't ever doubt yourself. 'Cause you know what? Haters gonna hate. They're not your problem, and like my son's teacher, they often don't even know what they're talking about.

I finished my story and told my friend that people will always judge or criticize us, but that she shouldn't be so quick to listen to them instead of her own instincts. Why would you let other people decide your choices or dreams? If you don't believe in yourself, who will?

What do you think some of the most successful people have in common? People thought they were going to fail. Instead, they triumphed.

I asked her, "Besides, who's living your life?"

With that, she wiped her tears, raised her glass, and yelled, "I am! And I'm not giving up!"

Questions: Who's Living Your Life?

Did the story remind you of a time when you let someone else's opinion affect your life and the decisions you wanted to make? Who was it?

How did that make you feel?

What decision did you initially want to make?

Do you still let other people's opinions dictate your life decisions? If so, why?

There will always be times when others will have an influence over you—we are human, after all. However, if you are being swayed to think, say, or do things you don't agree with, then you need to take action and stand up for yourself. Are you ready to start living your life?

"It's better to lose your ego to the one you love than to lose the one you love because of your ego."

~ Unknown

Free Pass

Friday night. 12:45 a.m. I'm heading home after a fabulous evening with my best girlfriend. I hop into an Uber, rest my head back, and close my eyes. It's been a long day.

"You have a good night tonight?"

I open my eyes and meet my driver's gaze in the rear-view mirror.

"Amazing," I say. "How about you?"

He must be dying to talk to someone, because within minutes I learn all about him, including the fact that he's a young, exhausted parent with a toddler and an infant waiting at home. I can't help but giggle as memories of raising children flood into my mind. I could definitely relate.

I told him about the epic temper tantrums, the mulish stubbornness, the loud screams of "NO!" that I can still hear ringing in my ears. The driver laughs, nods his head.

He tells me it's nice to meet another parent club member. Someone who understands. He asks how old my kids are.

"Nineteen and twenty," I tell him. "Both boys."

He runs his hand through his hair, shaking his head in disbelief. I can see that his eyes are wide.

"How . . . did you get through it?"

My mind flashes back, a lifetime condensed into bullet points: Hormones. First love. Heartbreak. Marriage. Motherhood. Long talks. Late nights. The good times. The bad. How did I get through it?

All I can do is laugh. I say, "It won't be easy, but it'll be worth it."

He asks if I have any advice. I can hear something in his voice, almost desperation.

I feel for him. I can remember so clearly what it was like in the beginning. Years of being sleep deprived and overwhelmed, praying the next stage would get easier. I took every bit of advice I could get, ate it up like a starving animal. As I search my mind for something to say to him, one incredible memory jumps forward, and I decide to share it.

As a parent, one of my biggest fears is that as my children grow into adults, they'll drift away and we'll no longer be close. I was always aware of this, being that I'm not close with my own parents. I never wanted this to be my future. Our future.

When my eldest son was around thirteen, it was one of the toughest times for me as a mother. Starting puberty and high school, my eldest embraced his new-found maturity and independence with gusto. Peach fuzz above the lip, a deeper voice, and a social life that was free of Mom and Dad.

One day during exam season, he texted me after school to tell me he was going to hang out with his friend, John, and wouldn't be coming home until later. I texted him back. No. You're not allowed. You need to come home and study. You'll have plenty of time for friends after this is all over.

He quickly responded: I'm not coming home.

I sat and frowned at my phone for a minute. I could feel my insides coming to a boil. Did he honestly just send that? I collected myself, called him, and told him he needed to come home immediately. He disagreed, hung up on me, and turned off his phone.

In a word, I was livid! How dare he?

Without thinking I grabbed my keys, jumped in my car, and gunned it towards John's house. My ego was in the driver's seat now. As I clutched the wheel, my knuckles white, I yelled out, "I'm going to kill him! I'm . . . going . . . to . . . kill him." I devised the most thorough punishment my imagination could come up with. No video games, no cellphone, no friends. For a month. No, two months. No, six. In their place would be manual labour, solitary confinement, and whatever other misery I could inflict on him. By the time this was over, he'd be longing for the light of day.

But as I drove towards John's house, a sudden thought popped into my head. It scared me so much that I had to pull over. My son was drifting away, and if I didn't handle this right I might never get him back. What I feared the most was now right in front of me. I couldn't catch my breath. I started to cry.

I uttered out loud, "Help me, help me . . . Please give me an answer!" I don't know who I was asking. God? The universe? I don't know. All I knew is I needed help. I slowed down my breathing and searched my soul. Suddenly, a calm I'd never felt came over me.

I sat there for another minute, then put the car in drive and continued on my way to John's house. I was driving slower now. I had no idea what I was going to say when I got there, but for some reason I trusted the words would come when they needed to.

Feeling strangely comfortable, I rang John's doorbell. Michael was shocked when he saw me. He practically snarled, pushed past me, and stomped to the car with exaggerated anger. We both got in. I still didn't know what I was going to say.

He slammed his door, crossed his arms, and demanded I tell him what his punishment was. Looking defeated, he threw his cellphone into the middle console, knowing from past experience this was usually the first thing to get used against him.

Suddenly, I knew how I was going to handle this. I couldn't believe it. I looked at Michael and said, "You can have your phone back. I've decided not to punish you."

He looked at me in disbelief. Did he just win the lottery, or had his mother gone completely insane?

"I don't get it," he said.

To this day I still can't believe the words that came out of my mouth.

"You don't know this, Michael, but as a parent we're granted one free pass to give to our children when they screw up. The parent can make this decision any time they see fit. It doesn't matter how big or small the issue is, but when the decision is made we can't take it back. You only get one though."

I looked at Michael and watched his reaction. His face softened, his shoulders relaxed. He looked incredibly relieved. For a moment, that is. Then his relief turned into panic.

He grabbed my arm and said, "Mom, I can't have my free pass now! I'm only in grade nine and I feel like I am going to screw up a lot worse than this. Please don't use my free pass now!"

To my surprise and delight, he actually started begging for me to punish him. I couldn't believe what was happening.

In a very calm, even tone I explained to him that I'd made my decision and I couldn't take it back. That's the rule, kid. I decided today was the day, and that was that.

I pulled the car over and looked straight into his eyes. I said, "However, if you ever pull a stunt like that again you don't wanna know what your punishment will be. Enjoy your free pass, Michael."

Whatever that was, I think it worked. My son didn't pull away that day, and over the next few years we grew even closer. There were more difficult patches later on, of course, but our closeness let us navigate those rough waters with ease. To this day, our relationship keeps getting better and better.

Things could have gone very differently that day. I could have let my anger and ego push us apart. I could have punished him, only to perpetually relive the tug-of-war with him for years, driving a wedge between us. I'm so thankful I didn't.

The Uber driver pulls up in front of my house right as I'm finishing my story.

"Parent with love and not with your ego," I say.

He sighs and turns in his seat to look at me. Then he tells me that his own father had let his anger and ego parent him as a teenager. Now they hardly have a relationship.

Please remember this story I told him. Someday you might have a thirteen-year-old of your own, and you'll be tested just like I was. Enjoy your free pass. You won't get another.

Questions: Free Pass

What was your relationship like with your parents?

Believing our children's accomplishments and behaviours are a reflection of us is ego-based, which is why the power struggles exist. What will other people think or will I be judged? Did your parents believe this? Did your parents parent with ego?

What is your relationship like today?

Do you sometimes feel this way and find yourself parenting with ego?

Why do you feel you are parenting from ego? What are your concerns?

What is your relationship like with your children?

How would you rather react and parent your children? How can you start today?

"Sometimes letting go is simply changing the labels you place on an event. Looking at the same event with fresh eyes."
~ Steve Maraboli

I Choose the Roller Coaster

It always starts with a feeling. Something isn't right, and I can't figure out what. I'm so anxious I can barely sit still. It keeps me up at night, pacing and pondering. Days pass, but the feeling does not. And then all of a sudden, the answer will come to me.

The situation is always different but the conclusion I reach is always the same: I need to make a change. A big one. Some call it intuition. I've followed it many times in my life, and it has never led me astray.

If there's one thing I've learned about myself, it's that sometimes I need to make radical changes in order to be truly happy. I have no choice. It can be really scary to leave a marriage or a highly successful career, but every time I've followed that feeling my life has transformed for the better.

That feeling has come back. It's tugging at my insides even as I type this.

When I launched the Positive People Army, it ignited a fire in me. I'd always known I wanted to make a difference and spread positivity, and the blog became how I would do that. Or at least a great start. I labelled it my Passion Project. As the weeks passed, more and more people started reading, sharing, and following. Some folks even decided to join in and submit their own stories.

The blog was flourishing. The army was growing. I should have felt pure joy. But the more the blog grew, the more angst I started to feel. Why did I feel this way?

Writing and sharing positive energy was exactly why I created the Positive People Army, and I was getting exactly what I wanted. So what was I missing?

It reminded me of something that happened when my eldest son was about to turn eighteen. As his birthday approached, a strange uneasiness began to come over me. I just couldn't put my finger on why. Then one day the answer came to me. Or rather, it was thrust into my face.

During an argument, my son actually yelled, "You're not the boss of me anymore!"

My heart sank, and I suddenly understood what had been making me so uncomfortable. It was the thought of his impending transition into adulthood. He was going from someone who needed his mother to someone who didn't.

Throughout Michael's life, I've tried my best to readjust and grow as a parent, but this particular circumstance was very different. Since the time he was born I had made every decision in his life. I picked the food he ate and the clothes he wore. I decided which school he went to and what extracurricular activities he would enjoy. In essence I was the manager of his life. It truly was the best job I could ever have asked for. But he no longer needed or wanted a supervisor.

I couldn't get his words out of my head. You're not the boss of me anymore. They echoed through my mind for days. After many sleepless nights, I finally admitted my discomfort to my husband. I told him how saddened I was to be losing Michael.

He looked at me sympathetically, held my hand, and said, "Sweetheart, you will never lose Michael—he loves you so much. You just need to readjust your role and probably give yourself a new title, and the two of you will be just fine."

His words hit me like a sack of bricks. He was right! Why had I thought I would ever lose my son? All I had to do was modify how I was parenting and give myself a new label.

With that thought I decided to retire as Manager of Michael's Childhood. I then gave myself the fancy new title, Consultant to His Adulthood. It has a nice ring to it, don't you think? And it was a simple change that worked. Michael is now twenty-two years old, and both of us have settled into our new roles quite well.

Remembering this moment helped me realize that maybe I needed help finding the answers, like my husband had helped me regarding Michael. A number of days later I ran into a wonderful friend I hadn't seen in a while. The moment she saw me she started gushing about the PPA. She shared her favourite stories and congratulated me on releasing such a positive force into the world. I blushed and thanked her for her kind words. Then I sighed and confessed that I was feeling some unease about it, but had no idea why.

We talked about how I felt writing the posts and how much it meant to me to receive others people's stories. She asked me what my hopes and dreams were for the Positive People Army. Then the most amazing thing happened. I got the answer. While I was speaking to her I unintentionally changed the mental label I had given the blog—from my Passion Project to My Life's Project.

The moment I said it I stopped myself. My entire body shuddered and I could feel goosebumps rising on my skin.

"Oh my God," I said to her. "I think I just discovered why I've felt so funny. I want the PPA to be more than just a hobby. I hadn't even realized this until I said it!"

My girlfriend laughed and said, "I guess you need to start figuring out what that means and get to work on making it a reality."

It's terrifying to admit something like this out loud, even more so to actually write it down. But I know deep down that if I don't, it won't happen. Without people knowing what I want, the opportunities will never be offered to me.

I struggled to write this story for almost a week, afraid to put it out there in the universe, but I just had to do it. And within twenty-four hours of writing the first draft, I was emailed and asked to do my first radio interview about the Army. The universe had answered me in record time. It was an amazing sign and an incredible start to this journey! Once again, making a mental change had made all the difference in the world.

I realize this won't happen overnight, and I could either be incredibly successful or fail miserably. The way I look at it, I need to decide what kind of life I want. Do I want my life to be a carousel, going around and around in a predictable pattern? Or do I want my life to be an unpredictable roller coaster ride, joyous, scary, and beautiful?

In my heart I know there's only one real choice. I choose the roller coaster, and I'm going to ride it with my hands up.

Watch out world, it's time for the Positive People Army to become a phenomenon.

Questions: I Choose the Roller Coaster

We all give ourselves many different labels in our lives. Who we are in our families, at work, within our friendships. How we define our success. What are some of the labels you have given yourself?

How do each of these labels make you feel?

Are there any labels you have given yourself that you are struggling with at the moment, or are there some that are preventing you from moving forward?

Sometimes other people give us labels based on our relationships or performances. What are some of the labels other people have given you? How do you feel about them?

Is there a label you would like to give yourself? Why?

"It's not the circumstances that create joy. It's you."
~ Unknown

A Plague of Joy

I've got this one friend who complains about everything. Work is terrible. Traffic is a drag. The weather is too cold. No wait. Too hot. Why doesn't this place have Wi-Fi? She'll always find something. Every day. She's very good at it.

Sometimes it seems like she's taking life way too seriously, and it's drained all the joy she should be savouring, as if her negativity is a bear trap clamped around her ankle. I'm not judging her or anything. I used to let myself be a lot like her, until one ludicrous event changed everything.

This was years ago, when my sons were still little. It was Friday at the end of a really, really long week. Mike and I were going to have friends over for dinner and a glass or two of wine. Definitely two.

Just as I was leaving work, Mike texted me to say he had to stay late at his job, which meant I was now on my own to get everything ready for our dinner party. Already running really late myself, I could feel the frustration brewing as I drove to pick up Haydn and Michael from school.

I rushed them into the car and informed them we were making a few stops before heading home, and that they needed to help me tidy the house. Both of them started whining immediately. I turned and pointed a threatening finger at them, giving them fair warning that I was not in the mood to listen.

They crossed their arms and sulked. Michael even whispered under his breath, "This sucks!"

I agreed with him.

For the next hour I dragged the boys from one place to the next. The more I needed them to hurry, the more distracted and silly they became. I told them to cut it out, but they didn't seem to hear me that day. My patience was wearing thin.

Just as we finished our last errand, the boys reminded me that we needed to stop at the pet store to pick up crickets for their beloved bearded dragons (giant lizard pets). I had promised I would the night before. And they were right. I had. But in the frenzy of the day, I'd completely forgotten.

"Fine, but we need to be fast," I said, and we raced to the pet shop.

Fifteen minutes later, we were back in the car with some new passengers. One hundred live crickets in a clear bag. I pulled into the driveway with only forty-five minutes left to unpack the car, clean the house, and set the table before my guests arrived. I wasn't sure I was going to make it.

I started barking orders at the boys like a drill sergeant, but all they were focused on was pouring the crickets out from the plastic bag and into the top of the little cricket keeper thing that held them until their doom when they would be fed to the lizards.

My annoyance started to soar, and I yelled at them to hurry up, but to do so carefully. They didn't hear that last bit. I don't really know what happened, but the next time I looked up, a hundred crickets were jumping all over my kitchen, chirping chaotically, suddenly everywhere.

I screamed and scrambled up onto a chair to get away from them. My frustration exploded, and rage suddenly gripped my senses. I could feel myself about to start yelling in a way I rarely do. But then the most amazing thing happened. As I watched Haydn and Michael frantically trying to capture the crickets, it was like time slowed down, and I saw the situation clearly for the first time.

My sons were running around like lunatics, screaming with laughter. I can only describe it as pure joy, and it was an amazing thing to watch. In that split second, I realized I had two choices. I could continue feeling annoyed and angry, or I could just let go and enjoy this ridiculous moment for what it was. I chose joy.

Laughing uncontrollably, I jumped off the chair and started chasing crickets with the boys. They were everywhere! Every time we tried to put a cricket into the keeper, another one would jump out. It was like a comedy routine. We squealed with excitement and pretty much had the time of our lives.

It took us about fifteen minutes to get all of the little guys into their box. Once we were done, my boys enthusiastically helped me get ready for the dinner. We were all in such a fabulous mood.

Mike got home with ten minutes to spare. Anticipating the cold shoulder for leaving me to deal with everything myself, he was pleasantly surprised to hear about our cricket adventure. Also, our dinner party guest found it hilarious when we kept hearing a rogue cricket chirp throughout the evening. In fact, for weeks after I could still hear chirping from some crickets that had evaded capture. It always made me giggle.

That moment is a constant reminder to me that I should never let frustration take away from being happy and enjoying life. We can all get stuck in a negative rut from time to time. It's easy. Things go wrong, and there's nothing we can do about that. But we do have the power of deciding how we're going to react to things, and how we're going to let them make us feel.

Next time you're feeling that negativity bubbling up inside of you, just chill, take a few deep breaths, and try to think of something that makes you happy. You'll find something if you just try. Wouldn't you rather laugh than complain?

Choose to be happy. Choose joy. It's always your choice.

Questions: A Plague of Joy

Did the story remind you of a time when you regret lashing out negatively instead of choosing joy or happiness?

If so, why did you react negatively?

How do you generally react to stressful situations? Is your go-to response generally frustration, anger, or sadness?

If your response is generally negative, how would you rather react? Why?

How do you feel you could change your reactions from a negative response to a more positive one?

What is one action you could implement to make sure you respond in a more positive manner?

CHAPTER 5

Friendship

There is nothing quite as special as true friendship. In my life, I've had many different friends: best friends, close friends, and lots of acquaintances. All have been an important part of my life. My friends have taught me how to forgive, laugh, and take time to enjoy incredible conversations. All while still providing a safe emotional space for me to be myself.

Yet sometimes we often take for granted the importance of friends and the lessons we can learn from having their connection. Throughout this chapter, I explore some of my complex relationships and the significant lessons many of them have brought me.

"There are some people in life that make you laugh a little louder, smile a little bigger, and live just a little bit better."
~ Unknown

You'll Never Believe Who I Heard from Today!

A friend of mine has an impressive collection of shoes and bags. It's fabulous. We were talking about it a few months back, and she asked me if I collected anything myself. My first instinct was to say I don't, but as I took a moment to think about it, I suddenly realized that I do collect something.

"I collect friends," I answered.

She gave me a puzzled look. "That's not a collection," she said. "We've all got friends."

For days I thought about my statement. I collect friends. Was this an odd response, or could I actually call my friends a collection?

I don't know, but I believe everyone comes into my life for a reason, and if we make a connection even once they're in my life forever. Or I guess I should say, "in my collection." I have friends who are younger and friends who are older. Some are really successful; others are starving artists. And of course, I've got a few lost souls in my collection as well.

It doesn't matter who they are or what they do, I honestly feel like I'm close with all of them. I really do! That doesn't mean I get to see them all regularly, as nice as that would be. But whether I see someone every few days or every few years, we always pick up right where we left off when we finally come together.

Almost every day, my husband hears the same phrase: "You'll never believe who I heard from today!" Even after fourteen years of marriage, he never ceases to be amazed by the commitment I have towards every single person in my life, and how insanely busy our social lives can be. I just can't imagine not making time for someone after I've made a connection with them. I'd never want to miss out on our next conversation or experience.

You're probably reading this and thinking it's impossible to stay connected all the time, but it's not! One of the easiest ways I stay connected is by reaching out to someone as soon as a memory of them pops into my head. This happens all the time. Maybe the smell from a bakery makes me think of that amazing brunch I had with one friend, or a song on the radio reminds me of a concert where I met another. Any time that happens, I take it as a sign that this person needs to be in my life at that moment.

Perfect example: The other day, as I was leaving for work, I grabbed a gorgeous black and white circle scarf that I hadn't worn in a couple of years. The moment I placed it around my neck, a memory suddenly sparked in my mind and I started laughing out loud.

Many years ago, I was travelling for work and had the privilege of doing so with one of my dearest friends. On one of our rare days off, the two of us headed to a nearby mall to shop and catch a movie (pretty much the only thing you do when living on the road). It was during this outing that I bought the circle scarf.

Exhausted from shopping, we went to see the movie *Silver Linings Playbook* with Jennifer Lawrence and Bradley Cooper.

And I'm so glad we did. In the film's climactic dance scene, Jennifer leaps up onto Brad's shoulders, and as he clumsily twirls her around, her crotch ends up in his face. It's an incredibly awkward and funny scene, but not nearly as enjoyable as what happened next.

Completely dying of embarrassment for the characters, my friend buried her face into my shoulder and started slapping my arm, yelling, "No! No! No!"

So of course, I began laughing hysterically at her reaction. And I have a very loud laugh, which made everyone in the theatre turn around to scowl at our disruptive behaviour. Such an amazing moment!

Now you can see why putting on the scarf made me laugh. I texted her that day, and we had an amazing conversation reliving that moment, laughing about it all over again. It was such an easy and wonderful connection.

And it goes both ways. Not a day goes by that I don't hear from one of the hundreds of friends that I have. They could be a close friend or someone I haven't heard from in years. It could be just to say hi, or to ask for some advice, or for dozens of other reasons.

For me, it doesn't matter what the reason is. It always feels amazing, and I do my absolute best to get back to every one of them.

I created the Positive People Army to help people connect and support each other, to share the moments that define their lives, happy and sad alike. But I don't want people to forget that they already have their own army. Nurture your collection and it will nurture you.

If you don't connect with your network on a regular basis, try this: Every day or every week pick one person and send them a note. Try my trick and share a memory you have about them. You'll see how wonderful it feels to reconnect with someone, even if years have passed.

Do it. Right now! Start making more memories today. And get more out of the ones you've already got.

Questions: You'll Never Believe Who I Heard from Today!

Did the story remind you of an amazing moment you experienced with a friend? What was the moment and who was the friend?

When was the last time you reached out to them or saw them?

How do you generally stay in touch with friends?

Do you make a point of staying in touch with friends, or has life gotten in the way?

Who would you like to talk to right now if you could? What's stopping you?

Are you going to reach out to them?

"Best friends are like bras: close to your heart
and there for support."
~ Unknown

Lucky Charms Aren't Just for Kids

For years people have carried around lucky charms to bring
them good luck: a lucky rabbit's foot or a found four-leaf
clover. Are they really lucky or is this just a belief—and does it
really matter?

I have mentioned in a previous story that I attract people who
are "lost souls." I have never searched for this particular type of
person, they just always find me. One of the only explanations
I have is that I am a very animated, positive person, and I feel
they want to be surrounded by this type of energy. It doesn't
matter what the reason, I just love listening, helping, or holding
their hand.

I'm not a therapist or expert in any way, but in most cases,
people just want to be heard. However, sometimes when a person decides to talk about their pain, it feels as though this energy
has been transferred to me. Some people call this empathic.

This part is hard to explain, but anyone who has listened
to a hurting friend or family member knows the feelings they
are left with once they leave. Not only have I listened to people going through a hard time, many people have stayed with

my family if they needed to. Our home has always been a safe haven for many going through a difficult situation in their lives.

My eldest son seems to have inherited the "lost soul attraction gene" as well, which means a few of his friends have lived with us for months at a time in the past. I have always done my best to navigate the different energies in our house, but one particular house guest was a whole different story.

A very dear friend of ours tried to take his life. He was found in time, but the days that followed were overwhelming. Not really having a huge support system, he had nowhere to recover and heal. It became very clear to me he needed to come and stay with our family. Once again, we opened our home to another lost soul.

Quickly I could feel how much pain our friend was in and what he was going through. It was a dark energy inside him, one I had truly never encountered before. In the weeks that followed, I noticed my energy was shifting. It was nothing he was doing intentionally; he was just trying to share and heal, but for me this was becoming an issue.

Sadness, anger, and darkness were starting to consume me. My sunny, energetic personality was slowly disappearing, and I felt like I was losing control of my own emotions. Everyone at one time or another can relate to this because we encounter those people who feel good to be around; they improve your mood and vitality. Others are draining; you instinctively want to get away. This subtle energy can be felt inches or feet from your body and is very apparent when it happens.

Thank God I have such an amazing husband and friends who recognized that I was on the verge of an emotional breakdown.

After many tears and supportive conversations with friends, I realized I had left myself very unprotected from such strong emotions. It was time to find my force field again!

I've always been a spiritual person and truly believe in the power of rocks, gems, and crystals as a healing and protective source. The rock recommended to me for dealing with this particular situation was angelite. I carry it everywhere with me, and I truly feel its protective force field energy. Like the lucky rabbit's foot or the found four-leaf clover, it works!

It honestly doesn't matter to me if it really has energy or if it's a psychological thing. My point is, we all experience each other's energy, and we need to be aware of what is actually happening. Having a support system is key, and for some, like me, you may also need a lucky charm or positive stone to feel protected and safe.

This is why I created the Positive People Army to become the support system for anyone needing it. This community is not just for people going through something, but for people supporting someone as well.

Our house guest and I talked at great length about what we both went through, and we became very mindful of how our energies were affecting each other. In fact, he even started wearing a crystal quartz I bought him, a stone that has been called a master healer, and he felt stronger and protected because of it.

Again, it doesn't matter what your beliefs are . . . you just need to create your support system and believe in something to get you through this crazy life.

Questions: Lucky Charms Aren't Just for Kids

Have you ever noticed other's people's energy before? Positive or negative?

Do you find yourself affected by other's people's energies? Good or bad?

How do you deal with the energy experience?

Do you carry protective lucky charms or use visualization to help with the negative energies? What do you carry or visualize?

*"Until we have seen someone's darkness,
we don't really know who they are. Until we have forgiven
someone's darkness, we don't really know what love is."*
~ Marianne Williamson

I Felt Betrayed

If I were to describe myself, I'd say I'm a sensitive, caring person—someone who wears her heart on her sleeve. When I was younger, I thought these traits were a weakness. They made me vulnerable, easily taken advantage of, and frequently hurt. I tried to hide this part of me deep down. But the older I got, the more I realized that being emotional and compassionate wasn't something to be ashamed of or to shy away from. I needed to appreciate and embrace this side of me. It's what makes me . . . me.

I'm grateful that people feel comfortable sharing their problems and heartaches with me. I love listening, helping, or just being their shoulder to cry on. It's not something I do for praise or gratitude. I just love knowing I was able to make a difference in someone's life. It's a special feeling, one I cherish.

As I mentioned in the last story, a dear friend was at his lowest emotional point and needed a safe haven to rest, recover, and nurse his wounds. Without hesitation, I opened my heart and home, and he moved in with us. Weeks turned into months, and it became clear that living with my family was really helping him. He was growing stronger, more like his old self every day.

His outlook was getting better, and his life seemed a lot less bleak to him than it once had. His gradual recovery was inspiring.

And then, one day, he just left.

Some call it ghosting. It's something you might do at parties or when you're leaving a bar. It's definitely not something you do when you've lived with someone for four months, relying on them almost completely. He'd given no notice, no warning, that this was about to happen. Someone we'd supported like family and made a priority in our lives was gone. Just like that. We got a very impersonal email from him after, and that was all.

I felt betrayed, unappreciated, and cast aside—robbed of any pleasure that helping him had given me. Just like our friend, that special feeling had vanished. I was heartbroken. I barely slept for two nights. I was upset that I had let myself get hurt again. Had I opened myself to this with my desire to help every lost soul who crossed my path?

Now I wanted nothing more than to close my heart, lock everyone out forever. No matter how much love or support they needed, I wasn't letting them in. Tucked away in my emotional fortress, nobody could ever hurt me again. Sad and tired from my second sleepless night, I headed to the kitchen for some coffee. As I waited for it to brew, I looked out the patio door at my lifeless, desolate backyard consumed by winter: the trees bare, the furniture wrapped in tarps, the flowers long dead.

Staring out, lulled by the sound of my coffee trickling into the mug, my mind started to drift to memories of my stunning garden in the summer. My backyard is absolutely beautiful during the warmer months. It has multiple areas to entertain and relax, lush gardens that burst with colour, and lots of trees, which are strategically placed to add shade and privacy.

It's taken my husband and me eleven years to create this oasis. We planted and built every bit of it ourselves—the pond and the trees, the bushes and the structures. Every single patio stone was placed there by our own hands. It's been a labour of love that I truly enjoyed.

I thought about the rhododendron bush, which always blooms first in the spring. Shortly after, the peonies would flower, the trees would be adorned with leaves, and vibrant life would return to my garden once again. It wasn't dead, just dormant. It would flourish and prosper as if winter never happened. And in that moment, I realized my heart was no different. Winter melts into spring, bringing a season of new life. And like the winter, this feeling would pass.

So why had I been so quick to think I would never want to open my heart again? The possibility of getting hurt is never enough reason to not help someone. I can't let one person change me like that. I will never turn away a friend in need. In time I will forgive, forget, and move on. My heart will bloom again. With that thought I turned away from the door and grabbed my coffee. Walking to my couch, I could already feel the season turning.

Questions: I Felt Betrayed

Have you ever felt betrayed? What happened?

How did you deal with the betrayal?

Are you still holding on to the pain, or have you forgiven?

If you haven't let go and forgiven, what is stopping you?

Forgiveness is a conscious, deliberate decision to let go of the feelings of resentment or vengeance towards a person or persons who have hurt you, regardless of whether they actually deserve your forgiveness. Are you ready to let go of the pain and forgive?

If you were able to forgive, how would you do it?

How do you think you would feel if you were able to forgive?

> "Spread love everywhere you go. Let no one ever come
> to you without leaving happier."
> ~ Mother Teresa

A Simple Gesture

Sometimes one simple moment can make you look at your life completely differently. For me, this moment was a simple gesture for another person. It was my aha moment.

There's a local jazz bar that my husband and I love to go to every now and then. We'll go on random Saturday afternoons, have a couple of drinks, and take in some great live music. We've been going for years. We've gotten pretty friendly with the manager there, and even though we don't stop by very often, he always remembers us. A couple of years ago, he mentioned that his birthday was coming up, and for no particular reason my husband made a note of it.

Two years later, the alert popped up on my husband's phone. It was the manager's birthday. Since I'm always looking for any excuse to enjoy a glass of wine and some live music, I suggested we head over to the jazz club to wish the man a happy birthday. The place was busier than we'd ever seen it. The staff was slammed, just barely keeping up. We spotted the manager and saw he was practically run off his feet. However, he noticed us right away and warmly welcomed us back.

He scurried from table to table in an effort to keep up with the crowd. Most of the clientele didn't converse with him much, just pointed at their glasses for refills or made a checkmark motion in the air when they were done for the day. Don't get me wrong; some people were nice, but others were extremely rude. That's something you sort of come to expect when you live in a big city, but you never fully get used to it. The manager just went about his business.

The band finished their set, and most of the venue cleared out. As my husband and I sat at the bar and finished our drinks, the manager came over and asked if we wanted the bill.

"We'll have one more," I said. "And we want to buy you one, too."

"Why?" he asked, clearly puzzled.

"Well, we just wanted to wish you a happy birthday."

What happened next was truly amazing to watch! His whole demeanor changed as joy and amazement flooded his features. Right before my eyes, I saw him transform from someone who felt invisible to someone who felt like the king of the world. He just couldn't believe that two people he barely knew would go out of their way to wish him a happy birthday. Even customers who'd been coming for twenty years hadn't remembered, or most of his family, for that matter. He felt overwhelmed with gratitude for this simple act.

I've always wanted to make a difference in this world. Yet watching the manager's reaction that day left me speechless and truly changed. I realized that making a difference doesn't need to be a big production. Sometimes all you need to do is make another person feel recognized, make them feel like they matter.

To this day I cry every time I think of this special moment. We're all searching for our mission, our reason for being on this planet. I feel like this moment confirmed just how important my mission to make a difference is. And it happened with such a simple gesture. This is something we can all do. Let's make the world a better place. Together!

Questions: A Simple Gesture

Has someone ever done a simple gesture for you that made a difference in your life? What was the gesture?

How did it make you feel?

Did you ever tell that person how the gesture affected you?

Have you ever done a simple gesture for someone and had no idea the impact it would have on them? What did you do?

How did they react?

How did it make you feel?

CHAPTER 6

Life and Death

Everyone deals with life and death differently. Some share and express it, whereas others choose to ignore and deny the emotions altogether.

Yet as long as you are living, something wonderful could happen at any moment. Yes, life may still have its lows, but it will also always have its highs. It's a continual process of struggle, transformation, and growth.

Throughout this chapter I focus on the opportunities life and death grant us: the chance to create a fulfilling existence with purpose and meaning.

Life is brief. I hope my stories will help you always remember to embrace what every experience offers you and to spread a little magic.

"Enthusiasm makes ordinary people extraordinary."
~ Unknown

Ordinary to Extraordinary

My dreams and goals are never going to happen! My life is dull. I think I'm in a rut. Do you recognize these statements?

You should, because we've all said these exact words or something similar to ourselves at one time or another. In fact, you may be repeatedly saying something comparable to yourself right now. Take a deep breath. It's okay!

What you're actually experiencing is what I like to call the ordinary phase. I've labelled this stage with a common, almost uninteresting description because it honestly feels and looks this way. Yet without this stage, nothing can become more interesting, exciting, or most of all, extraordinary.

What most people don't realize is that this is the time when all the magic actually occurs. Life has to be ordinary to ever be extraordinary. It's actually no different from planting a flower seed. You see, I absolutely love gardening, and every spring I always plant new flower seeds in my yard. I'm always thrilled when they bloom and fill my yard with colour and beauty, but I never enjoy waiting for them to grow. I hate the ordinary phase.

In the first few weeks, I'm constantly checking the soil for growth, but I'm always disappointed when it seems like nothing is happening. However, below the black, dark soil, alone and out of sight, things aren't slow at all. What was once just a minuscule seedling has now fought to expand into a little sprout, using everything possible—the soil's nutrients, the sunshine, and the rain—to assist with its beautiful growth. The seed is gathering everything it needs to undergo a complete transformation.

A few weeks later, the seed's diligence and hard work pay off, and a tiny shoot breaks through the soil. I'm always overjoyed to finally see something happening. Within days, growth progresses quickly and a tall stem and tiny leaves appear. Nonetheless incredible, the next stage becomes slow and arduous again.

For days I watch intently to see if a flower will appear, but nothing seems to be happening. Yet what I don't realize is my little plant is growing bigger and stronger every day in preparation for what is about to occur. Then without notice, a small colourful bud appears. What was once just a seed has begun to evolve into something remarkable. Nevertheless, it finally occurs—everything I've been waiting for. The bud blooms into an impressive, colourful flower. It becomes extraordinary.

Just like the flower seed, we must also experience every ordinary stage to succeed at what we want. In the beginning, it's exciting to set a goal and decide to make it happen. Once the initial excitement wears off and the work begins, the process can feel painstakingly slow, confusing, and hard. You may even want to give up. However, this growth stage is necessary and imperative for anything in life to happen. It's when you need to lean into the growth, learn, and collect everything necessary for your first transformation to begin.

The seed used the soil's nutrients, the sunshine, and the rain to help it grow. Without them, the seed never would have seen the light of day. For you, time is needed for research, lessons, mistakes, setbacks, and meeting all the necessary people to help propel you forward. This phase can often feel overwhelming, but without this initial growth, you will never break through the soil to see real potential and begin your transformation.

As things start to progress and your stem and leaves start to take shape, a new sense of excitement encourages you to keep going. However, even during this time, life can feel stagnant and, dare I say, ordinary. Sometimes this next growth period can take months, if not years, to properly yield any results, no different from the plant taking time to grow its leaves and stem before eventually revealing a bud and then a magnificent flower. Just like my flower didn't grow overnight, your dreams, goals, and life aspirations won't happen immediately, either.

Any worthwhile dream never happens immediately. Change is the result of small actions that contribute to a result over time. Just because you don't see anything happening and life feels boring and ordinary, it doesn't mean nothing is happening. Growth is always occurring.

When you can believe in the ordinary, holding strong to your journey and never giving up, ordinary will inevitably always become extraordinary, and with that, my friends, your flower will inevitably bloom.

Questions: Ordinary to Extraordinary

Are you a big dreamer?

Can you relate to the ordinary stage?

Are you going through it right now?

How does the ordinary stage feel? How would you describe it?

How do you generally handle the ordinary phase? Do you give up or keep plowing through it?

If you always give up during the ordinary stage, do you feel now you could keep going after realizing it's necessary?

What is one thing you are going to do differently next time during the ordinary stage?

"Grief is like the ocean; it comes in waves, ebbing and flowing. Sometimes the water is calm and sometimes it is overwhelming. All we can do is learn to swim."

~ Vicki Harrison

It Just Takes Time

Heidi, can you meet at the end of the day?" an incoming text read.

"Of course, is everything okay?"

"Yes, I actually have amazing news," my friend typed in all caps.

Her message was actually worrisome. The last number of months had been extremely difficult for her after tragically losing someone she loved. Overwhelming sadness and unpredictable anger consumed her most days. Yet lately I'd noticed she'd started covering up her sorrow with a happy hysteria. I worried the combination of heartache, frustration, and exhaustion was taking its toll on her.

Arriving at the restaurant, I was hesitant but pleasantly surprised when I saw sparkling wine on the table and my excited friend waiting. She actually seemed more like her old self. The moment I sat down, she couldn't hold the news in anymore and shrieked, "I got a promotion at work!"

"Congratulations," I screamed, enthusiastically raising my glass. I was thrilled to hear she finally had some good news in her life.

For the next hour we chatted about her new position and future plans. She seemed genuinely happy. Yet after a visit to the ladies' room, the all-familiar somber, sad, and grieving friend returned. The evening was turning more into a Dr. Jekyll and Mr. Hyde flick than a girlfriend get-together.

"Did something happen?" I asked.

"No, nothing happened. But I should feel ecstatic. I just don't understand. It seems like no matter how hard I'm trying to move on and have fun again, sadness keeps creeping back in."

My heart ached for her. I knew this agony all too well and felt it was time for me to share a story with her. When my kids were much younger, we owned a beautiful English bulldog we called Chansey. Our youngest son, Haydn, had named her after a Pokémon character. Her stature and bark could be intimidating, but in reality, she was a big old teddy bear. We adored and loved her.

When Chansey was three, our family decided to put a swimming pool in the backyard. From the moment they broke ground to the days that followed, we all watched from behind a construction fence like enthusiastic spectators at the zoo. It wasn't long before the pool was starting to take shape.

Three weeks later the safety fence came down, and I received a call at work that the pool was finished and officially open. It felt like Christmas morning! We were all dizzy with excitement to take the inaugural swim. As we arrived home, we all ran in separate directions like a mad flurry of chaos. Mike dashed into the kitchen to get dinner started. The boys ran to the basement feverishly in search of their new pool toys, and I ran upstairs to grab bathing suits and towels.

Digging around the boy's dresser drawers, I could hear Mike yelling for the dog downstairs. I didn't think much of it and continued rustling through bedroom drawers for suits. Then I heard Mike calling again: "Chansey . . . Chansey . . . CHANSEY!" His tone seemed a little more serious now.

A little worried, I ran downstairs to investigate what all the hollering was about.

"I can't find Chansey," Mike frantically said, as we locked eyes.

"Oh my God, you don't think she got outside do you?"

Mike's complexion turned pale white. "She can't swim," he gasped and sprinted out the backdoor towards the pool.

I just stood there frozen in my tracks, praying Mike would find her wandering around the yard. Then my worst fear came true.

"God, NOOOOOO," Mike screamed.

A splash echoed throughout the yard as Mike dove to the bottom of the pool. Chansey was gone. We closed the pool the next day. We never swam in it that season. The weeks that followed Chansey's death were heartbreaking. We missed everything about our beloved Chansey: her excitement when we arrived home, her silly playfulness, and even her deadly farts. Our home felt sad, quiet, and terribly unhappy.

Desperate for all of us to feel better, we impulsively purchased a pup and called her Emily. The first few days were fun. It felt great to have a dog in the house again. However, as the weeks passed, sadness re-emerged and our feelings towards Emily changed. It didn't matter how hard we tried to love her, she was a bandage covering up what we didn't want to feel. We didn't want another dog. We missed and wanted Chansey back.

Eventually we knew what we needed to do and found a wonderful new family for Emily. It broke our hearts to give her away, but we knew it was the right decision. The problem with placing a Band-Aid on a wound is it doesn't heal when it's always hidden away. Wounds need time and to be out in the open air for a scab to form and the recovery process to take place. It took us two years to heal before we were ready to adopt another dog.

Now it's been eleven years since we brought our bulldog Abby home, and a few years later, Hailey, a mixed breed, joined our family—two amazing dogs we may never have met if we didn't realize we were trying to cover up our grief with a quick fix.

Now sitting in the restaurant, I suggested to my friend that she shouldn't be so hard on herself. The loss of a loved one is like a tattoo on the heart. Permanent. Forever. Grief, however, is not. Don't postpone, deny, or run from it. Don't cover it up. Allow it and be with it. The sooner you accept it, the sooner it will pass.

It really will come to an end. It will just take time.

Questions: It Just Takes Time

Have you lost someone in your life? Who was it?

How did you handle your grief? Did you run from it or give yourself time to heal?

How long did it take you to heal?

What advice would you give to someone who is grieving?

If you haven't healed, do you feel it's time?

What do you feel you could do to start the healing process? Be honest with yourself.

Do you feel you are ready to heal?

"Never waste an opportunity to express your love to someone, because another opportunity is something life can't promise."
~ Trent Shelton

It Made Me Feel Loved

Recently I attended a funeral for a friend. He was forty-nine—so young. Eleven short months after being diagnosed, he was gone.

Nothing felt quite real as I listened to his loved ones talk about what a remarkable man he was. They told stories of his warm heart, his sharp wit, and his intense loyalty to family and friends. The tears flowed faster than they could be wiped away, hearing those touching tributes. There were many laughs, too.

After the service, I attended a wake he would have loved. Family, good friends, plentiful food and drink. A band played some of his favourite rock classics. I couldn't help but notice "Space Oddity" and "Hotel California" in the mix, reminding me of a few others gone too soon and before their time.

Photo slide shows of his life played on every television. I reminisced with his friends and family, sharing many poignant and funny stories about the man we loved. It truly felt like a celebration of his life.

However, as I left that day, I had this peculiar feeling I couldn't shake, a vague discomfort I just couldn't put my finger on. For days, I couldn't stop thinking about the service. I kept thinking about the lovely words that were said, the strong feelings that were shared. Then it dawned on me why I felt so uncomfortable: all those beautiful sentiments, but he wasn't around to hear any of them. What a sad thought.

Had they ever shared just how they felt about him when he was still here? Did he even have a clue how much he was loved by the hundreds of people in that church—how important he was to them? These questions consumed my thoughts, and I started to think about my own life. Do any of us tell the important people in our lives what they mean to us? I do my absolute best to keep connected with everyone I know, but am I saying enough?

I can't imagine the heartbreak and regret of speaking at a loved one's funeral, knowing I never got to tell them how I truly felt. Then I started to wonder: How would someone react if I sent a message revealing how I feel? Would it make them feel uncomfortable? Would they think I was being over the top and dramatic, or worse yet, insincere? How would people honestly react to such a deeply emotional note? Then the universe answered my questions the very next day with an Instagram post.

Mary wrote: Years ago, I met a woman who changed my world. If you've been fortunate enough to meet her you'll know exactly what I mean. She's this ray of intoxicating sunshine—the kind of presence in a room that draws you to herself effortlessly, magnetically, like a fluttering moth to a lantern. She's addictive. She's authentic, opinionated, simultaneously simple and complex. In my youthful way, nearly a decade ago, I would ask myself, "What would Heidi do?" I wanted to be her when I grew up. But do you know what's even more amazing than growing up to become someone you admire? Growing up to become someone that THEY admire.

The post was about me!

There are no words to describe how I felt in that moment. It was overwhelming. It made me feel acknowledged. It made me feel important. It made me feel loved.

That was the answer I was looking for. It was now time for me to start sharing, to fully show my heart to all the people I love. How do you think your friends and family would feel if you told them how you really feel? I can tell you: amazing.

The things you say after someone has died could benefit them so much while they're still alive. So say them. Don't think about it . . . just do it. Before it's too late.

Questions: It Made Me Feel Loved

Who did you automatically think about after reading the story?

What would you say to them?

Will you reach out and tell them how you feel? If not, what is stopping you?

Is there someone who has passed and you never got to tell them how you feel?

What would you have said?

"The truth is that life is a terminal condition. We're all going to die, but how many of us will truly live?"
~ Kris Carr

86,400 Seconds

For a long time, I stood in front of my kitchen chalkboard and stared at the number I'd written there: 86,400. It was the number I'd been obsessing over for weeks now—the number of seconds in a day.

It all started with a simple quote I read somewhere: "You've got 86,400 seconds today. Have you used one to smile?"

I've got so many inspiring quotes rushing past on my various feeds every day, but for some reason this one made me really stop and think.

86,400.

86,400.

It seems like such a large number, but I'd already used up 600 seconds or so just standing there pondering the number itself. Poof. They were gone. Sand at the bottom of an unflippable hourglass.

I try my very best to live every moment to its fullest, but how many seconds had I wasted doing things I didn't want to do? How many seconds had I spent living like a drone, wishing for the day to be over before it had even begun? Thinking about it sent a wave of panic washing over me. All those precious seconds

I'd taken for granted, neglected, and that were now gone forever. Was I living half a life?

Shortly after, I went to Cuba for my family vacation, and I was determined to savour every one of my 86,400 seconds. I woke up every day with only one goal: live life to the fullest and don't waste a second. That might sound like two goals, but the two go hand in hand, don't you think?

So for four days I lived the best I've ever lived. We drank tropical cocktails under the Havana sun, toured the city in a convertible with the top down, and laughed so hard our stomachs hurt. It was a beautiful time in a beautiful place. But by the fifth day I could feel my anxiety starting to creep back in. This would all be over soon, and I'd have to return to my regular life. My half life. A sad thought, since I'd really gotten to like living a full one. Could I keep living my 86,400 seconds to the fullest back in reality? Was that even possible?

We went to a restaurant that night, and I immediately noticed a woman sitting alone at the table next to ours. Our eyes locked and she smiled at me. I smiled back. As we waited for our drinks to arrive, my boys reminisced about the amazing day we'd had. In our enthusiasm, all of us were talking over each other, recapping our favourite moments, laughing constantly. I looked over and noticed the woman was watching us and smiling.

Our drinks showed up, and as we looked over the food menu, there was a natural lull in the conversation. The solo diner took advantage of the silence and remarked, "You have a lovely family."

We thanked her. My husband looked at me and motioned his head towards her. I knew he meant *Should we ask her to join us?*

I nodded. Yes. Of course.

Mike extended the invitation to her. Without hesitation she said yes, grabbed her wine glass, and moved to our table. Her name was Nicole. She lived in Quebec and was travelling alone. She was lovely, and I immediately liked her.

Nicole was an avid traveller, and she dazzled us with stories of her escapades, which she told in such vibrant detail it felt like we were living every moment with her. Her energy was magical. We learned a lot about her. She'd done so much, her life packed with joy and adventure, most recently a whirlwind love affair with a beautiful dancer. The story was so exotic and glamorous, I wondered if she'd stepped out of the pages of a romance novel.

Her special charm was intoxicating to be around, and we hung on every word she spoke. Her zest for life was so vibrant, so youthful. So you can imagine our shock when she revealed that she was actually seventy years young. We all gasped! She chuckled at our reaction. This truly was a woman taking advantage of her 86,400 daily seconds.

I had to ask: "Nicole, what's your secret to living such an extraordinary life and embracing every moment like you do?"

"Oh, my friend," she said. "Life is not always champagne and fireworks. I've also experienced my fair share of sadness and struggle. I just choose to look at these moments as a doorway to understanding life. These uncomfortable emotions can empower you and help you see what really matters: kindness, love, and compassion.

"The way I look at it . . . life is terminal, and I just have to live every moment."

Then she picked up her wine glass, raised it in the air, and announced, "I may have more adventures behind me than ahead of me, but my answer is a renewed passport for ten more years!"

"To living life!" We all raised our glasses and drank.

Meeting her was such a gift that day. She helped me realize I wasn't wasting any seconds during times of struggle, doing things I didn't want to do. I needed to understand that these moments are crucial in shaping and guiding me towards my best life. Without these times, I won't become the person I need to be. Thank you, Nicole, for making me realize that I really am living 86,400 seconds every day!

So, I ask you, how are you spending yours today?

Questions: 86,400 Seconds

Do you feel you're living your 86,400 seconds?

Do you believe you can embrace every second to its fullest?

In times of struggle, are you leaning into your pain and learning what you can? Do you feel this helps you have a fulfilled life?

What would you like to do to live a more fulfilled life? Name one thing.

What can you do to make that one thing a reality?

CHAPTER 7

Experiences

I'm grateful to share I've had some pretty extraordinary life experiences. Moments of unbelievable pain and heartache as well as extreme joy and happiness.

Yet what I'm most proud of is that all my experiences taught me some of the most profound lessons and granted me the most incredible awareness. They have helped me to truly live my authentic truth.

This last chapter is filled with some of the most powerful life experiences I've lived to become the person I am today. I realize there are many more to come, and I'm ready with an open mind and open arms to receive them all.

I hope you are ready to do the same.

"She threw away all her masks and put on her soul."
~ Unknown

Traded My Mask for a Cape

We all have that one memory we describe as the best moment ever. For some, it's the day they met the love of their life, whereas others reminisce about monumental milestones like their wedding day or the birth of their children. All are generally lovely moments of joy and happiness.

I agree these memories were pretty phenomenal in my life, but for me, the most extraordinary moment happened sitting in a parking lot. Alone and staring at my phone. It wasn't a happy, magical instance. It was one of the bravest moments I have ever experienced.

For the majority of my life, I had convinced others that I was a courageous and invincible person. I had always been fearless, driven, outgoing, and I wouldn't let anything stop me from doing or saying what I wanted. Yet deep down, I always knew I had one cautiously kept secret: a carefully created façade that hid my vulnerability.

I had invented my disguise because I had persuaded myself that sadness, anxiety, and fear were liability emotions and signs of weakness and impotence—not in other people, just me.

The mere sighting of one of these vulnerable emotions would cause me to either retreat into solitude or strap on what I liked to call my virtual mask of denial: a piece of protective armour I imagined would help me pretend everything was all right. Both tactics had become amazing tools of denial, shielding me from ever feeling helpless, exposed, weak, or even worse—hurt. My emotional tactics had everyone, including myself, convinced I was perfect.

Flash-forward to that lonely parking lot. I had been summoned to appear in court with my ex-husband, yet again. Even though I had left my ex fifteen years earlier, he was still creatively finding ways to be vindictive and vengeful, and today was nothing different. On the drive to the courthouse, I could feel my fear and anxiety bubbling up.

Not now, I thought.

I started my denial regimen with a confidence pep talk— "You've got this, you're better than this"—followed by visually imagining my virtual mask of denial being comfortably placed on my face.

Yet once I arrived, every device I had put into place was quickly disintegrating. The thought of seeing my ex and starting another court battle put my stomach into knots, and a wave of nausea washed over me. I felt scared, overwhelmed, and defeated before I'd even begun. I slumped over the steering wheel and began to cry.

"I need help," I murmured to myself.

There was no denying it: my vulnerability was at an all-time high. It was at this time that panic set in. I know this sounds a bit dramatic, but I'd honestly convinced myself that life as I knew it would instantly crumble if I admitted my vulnerability. Even to myself. Yet nothing had happened. The sky had not fallen. The earth hadn't opened up and swallowed me whole. I hadn't died. Nothing had happened at all.

I repeated the words again. "I need help." Still nothing.

And yet, I couldn't help but notice that every time I repeated the phrase, the complete opposite of what I thought would happen happened: I felt relief.

With this new-found liberation, or maybe it was insanity, I grabbed my phone, opened my Facebook profile, and began to type a post: "Vulnerability is one of the hardest emotions for me, but today I've decided to be vulnerable and ask for everyone's help. I have to go up against one of the most negative human beings I know and I'm feeling anxious and scared. I'm reaching out to all my friends to help by sending positive intentions and vibes to help get me through this. I know I can do anything, but I don't want to do it alone!! Love you all!! xo"

Once I'd written it, I stared at my words. I had worked so hard my entire life to make sure no one ever saw this side of me, and now in one short paragraph I was willing to change everything. I took a deep breath . . . and pressed send.

What happened next felt like a miracle. Within minutes, my phone started buzzing with notifications. I couldn't look. Yet my phone wouldn't stop vibrating. Finally, after about a minute I picked up my phone and started to read the messages. I couldn't believe it! All were reassuring sentiments of love, positive energy, and support. Nobody judged my plea for help, nor did they criticize my fear. But most of all nobody disapproved or condemned my vulnerability.

I honestly didn't know what I'd expected, but it definitely wasn't this. Hundreds of supportive and encouraging messages flooded my phone. To say I was astonished is an understatement. Quickly my tears of sorrow turned into tears of gratitude and appreciation. What I had feared the most had just become my saving grace. It felt incredible!

I walked into the courtroom that day without any of my denial devices. I felt strong, powerful, like a new-found me. I won the court battle that day . . . in more ways than one.

For my entire life I'd believed that admitting my vulnerability was my greatest weakness. Yes, vulnerability can make me more susceptible to hurt, heartbreak, and disappointment—there's no denying that! But without allowing myself to be vulnerable, I was missing out on intimacy, close relationships, and personal growth. I wasn't experiencing life or my genuine self. By getting comfortable with being uncomfortable, I had finally discovered what true courage felt like and there was no going back after that. I'd cracked open my perfect façade, and it actually felt amazing.

From that day forward, I retired my virtual mask of denial, and I now wear a virtual courageous cape of vulnerability. Fighting and dealing with every emotion, like a true superhero would. For me, this day will always be one of my most memorable—the day I discovered not only what true bravery is but my authentic self as well.

Are you ready?

Questions: Traded My Mask for a Cape

Does vulnerability scare you? Are you someone who wears a mask?

Do you wear your vulnerability mask the majority of the time or only when dealing with certain emotions?

Describe when you wear your vulnerability mask.

Why do you feel you wear your vulnerability mask?

Are you ready to retire your vulnerability mask and wear a courageous cape?

What do you think it will take to get ready for the vulnerability mask?

"I haven't failed.
I've just found 10,000 ways that won't work."
~ Thomas Edison

I Made a Mistake

This couldn't be right. I ran our Jays tickets through the scanner again, but the message was the same: DECLINED. Written in big red letters so as to accurately convey the seriousness of the situation. I felt the blood rushing to my face. The people behind us started to mutter with impatience. *Okay. Stay calm, Heidi. Third time's the charm,* I thought as I tried again.

DECLINED. I couldn't believe what I was seeing. I squinted at the letters as if that would somehow change them. Blushing, I handed my tickets to the stadium employee. As she examined them, I still felt some hope that this would all work out. But when she looked up and met my eyes, I knew this was not going to be the case.

"Sorry, ma'am, but these tickets were for last night's game," she said, pointing to the date at the bottom of the ticket.

"They can't be!" I gasped, mortified.

But they were, my husband informed me, as he looked them over himself. Sheer embarrassment seized my insides, and I suddenly found myself lost in a storm of self-loathing. *What is wrong with me? How could I have made this mistake? Why didn't*

I double-check the dates? I've ruined our night! But then, as if whispered in my ear by an angel, a quote from one of my most beloved books leapt out at me: "A mistake is only a mistake if you repeat it. The first time, it's nothing more than a beautiful lesson."

A calm feeling washed over me. Thanks, Robin Sharma.

"Heidi . . . Heidi . . . Heidi!"

I snapped out of the trance I was in and realized Mike was trying to get my attention.

"What do you want to do?" he asked.

With a giant smile on my face I said, "I want to see the game. Let's go to the ticket window and buy some new tickets."

"Let's do it," he said without missing a beat.

As we were standing in the ticket line, I realized I really did learn a valuable lesson just then. The old Heidi would have spent countless hours analyzing the screw-up, beating herself up, nurturing all the disappointment, resentment, and guilt inside of her. But now I knew that holding on to something I couldn't change would only drag me down. Letting go of a mistake and moving on felt amazing. It was freeing. Then something kind of crazy happened.

"Are you looking for tickets?" a woman's voice asked from behind me.

I turned to her and said, "We are. Why? Are you selling them?"

"I was trying to sell them, but a few minutes ago, I decided to pay it forward and find two people I felt deserved them. I don't know what it is about the two of you, but you have such a great energy, I would like to give you my extra tickets," she explained.

"What?! Are you kidding me? You want to give us FREE tickets?"

"Yes, I do!" she exclaimed.

I was so shocked and amazed, I actually reached out and hugged this very generous stranger. Startled, she started laughing and gushed that she never expected anyone to react the way I did. She was dumbfounded by my appreciation.

Once we entered the stadium, we told our big-hearted new friend what had happened with our tickets. She was stunned. We all agreed it was a miraculous moment.

While watching the game, I couldn't help but reflect on what had just happened. Letting go of my mistake had resulted in one of the most memorable moments of generosity I have ever experienced. Lessons and signs are all around us every day. We can choose to ignore them or we can choose to listen and learn. Even when we make mistakes.

I'm truly grateful I listened that Friday night. This was one lesson and experience I will treasure forever. The Blue Jays were victorious that day, but in the end, I felt like I was the real winner.

Questions: I Made a Mistake

How do you handle mistakes? Do you beat yourself up or learn from them?

What was the last big mistake you made? How did you handle it?

How would you have liked to have handled it?

If you were to guess what the lesson was, what do you think it was?

Is there one mistake from your past that you still regret?

What do you think you were supposed to learn from it?

"When I let go of what I am, I become what I might be."
~ Lao Tzu

A Cyclone Hits Costco

Recently, a friend of mine chopped her hair shorter. She looks amazing! After I told her so, she admitted she totally regretted doing it and she'd gone through a "mini breakdown" for two days after leaving the salon.

I gave her a closer look, thinking she had a problem with the cut itself. She looked beautiful to me. When I asked her why she wasn't happy with it, she explained that all her life she'd had long, gorgeous hair, but recently she'd just felt like a change. She had no idea how cutting off her hair would make her feel. Awful, it turns out. Worse than that, it made her feel old.

Standing there, listening to her recount her breakdown, I realized she was describing a milestone moment in a woman's life. It's an emotional cyclone that can't be avoided—the realization your youth is now behind you.

I remember the day it happened to me. In fact, I don't think the Costco optometry department will ever forget it. I've always been the kind of person who celebrates every birthday with extreme enthusiasm. I've lovingly embraced every decade and never had a problem with the number of candles on my cake. I just felt proud to have made it to another year and rejoiced in all the great times and accomplishments that had gotten me to that point.

Honestly, it had never crossed my mind that I was actually getting older. Maybe that sounds naive, but it's true. Such a concept just hadn't occurred to me. I'd always found it fascinating when people complained about how old they were, how old they felt, and how they truly hated both of those things. I'd just never felt that way.

Then one day, during a regular checkup at the Costco optometry department, everything changed. I was about to be hit by a cyclone.

"Well, Heidi, your right eye is a little worse and needs a new prescription, but not to worry, your left eye seems to be the same. However, we do need to discuss adding a progressive lens to your prescription."

"What's a progressive lens?" I asked.

My optometrist explained that I needed reading glasses now, and the progressive lens would allow me to use one pair of glasses for both reading and distance. Wait. What? Did he honestly just tell me I needed reading glasses?

No. I heard him wrong. There's no way he just said that.

"I can't possibly need reading glasses," I said.

Then the fateful words were spoken. In a very clinical manner, he said, "You do need reading glasses. When you reach your age, it's inevitable."

"Excuse me? Reach my age?"

I could see by his startled reaction he suddenly realized he'd said a bad, bad thing. He tried to backpedal, make it better. It didn't work. Not amused, I grabbed my prescription and stormed off to order my hateful new glasses.

I could feel my emotions brewing. Within me, blue skies were turning grey, darker and more ominous by the second. A storm was coming. Waiting to order my glasses, I thought, *How did I get here? This couldn't be possible. How could I be someone who needed reading glasses? Only old people needed those . . .*

Then it hit me—a question almost too terrible to ask. *Am I old?* Oh no. The storm was here. The hurricane had made landfall.

In that moment, the salesperson asked, "Are you ready to order your glasses?"

The poor guy had no idea what was about to hit him. I handed him my prescription. He asked if this was my first time ordering progressive lenses. I nodded, barely able to focus on what was happening. With an inappropriately chipper tone, he explained the different levels of progressive lenses and asked me which level I wanted to order. The storm was raging now, ripping through buildings, tossing cars, and flooding streets. I put my head in my hands and started shaking it back and forth.

"How is this my life right now?!" I said it several times. Loudly.

"Uh . . . pardon me?" The sales associate sounded beyond confused.

I looked up at him. "Do I look like someone who needs reading glasses? How'd I wake up this morning feeling young, and now I'm being told I'm an old person who needs reading glasses? I can't handle this. This can't be happening!"

He just stared at me, dumbstruck, shocked. Frantic, I shot up from my seat and started looking across the store for my husband, Mike. When I saw him predictably browsing the electronics section, I started yelling his name. He could hear the hysteria in my voice. He locked eyes with me and hurried over, looking puzzled. I started crying, rambling about getting old. I sounded like a crazy person, out of control, like I'd snapped and there was no coming back.

Mike glanced at the salesperson, who was staring at him with a frightened look that seemed to say, "Please do something."

As a couple, Mike and I are the complete opposite of each other. As you may be able to tell, I'm maybe just a little bit dramatic, whereas Mike is very cool and laid-back. He's always been, and definitely was on this day, the calm to my storm.

Right away, Mike seemed to understand that an emotional cyclone had just touched down at Costco, and he needed to rescue me quickly. He got me to sit down. I looked up at him in complete desperation. He placed his hand on my shoulder, looked into my eyes, and calmly said, "Sweetheart, I completely understand what you're going through and how you feel right now, but I need you to focus and order your glasses."

"I can't," I whimpered.

Mike looked at me with the most understanding eyes and said, "Yes you can, Heidi, because once you've done that, you and I can leave Costco and you can be as dramatic as you want for the rest of the day."

I burst out laughing. I could feel the storm clouds clearing, blue sky starting to peek through again. I turned towards the sales associate and ordered my glasses. Then I stood up, hugged Mike, and whispered in his ear, "I'm going to be really dramatic now."

"I know," he said, stroking my hair.

Mike deserves a medal for that day!

One week later, I picked up my new glasses. I opened the case and stared at them. I realized the emotional cyclone I experienced was a reaction to losing someone I loved—my younger self. I placed them on my face and looked around. Suddenly everything was so clear—in so many ways. My youthful years were over, but I was beginning my next journey. I was terrified, excited, and thrilled to take on this next stage of my life, and I did it the only way I knew how: with zest, drama, and a spectacular pair of new glasses!

Questions: A Cyclone Hits Costco

Can you relate to the story?

Do you remember your milestone moment, saying goodbye to your youth? What happened?

How did you deal with saying goodbye, or are you still holding on to your youth?

Are you embracing this next stage of life?

If not, why?

*"Patience is not the ability to wait,
but how you act while you're waiting."*
~ Joyce Meyer

My War with Patience

Somewhere around the main course, our lovely dinner party experienced a minor hiccup. My girlfriend told us that a change in career and lifestyle had made her a more patient, happy person. I could see the transformation for myself. She really was calmer and more content than she used to be. I could relate, I said, having gone through a similar metamorphosis. Once restless and tremendously impatient, age had chilled me out, and my outlook was now far more laid-back, easygoing, and—dare I say—patient. A grating chuckle came from beside me. I turned to my husband and shot him a look.

"You've got to be joking," Mike said, the corners of his mouth rising just a bit.

I smiled, or tried to. In reality, it was probably a smirk at most. "Excuse me?"

"I'm sorry, sweetheart, but you're not patient. In fact, you get impatient just saying the word *patient*."

"What?!"

ME? Not patient? I was about to lose it.

Thankfully, I caught myself, realizing this wasn't the time or place, and quickly changed the subject. The rest of the dinner was amazing, and we had a great evening with some old friends.

However, as I lay in bed that night, I couldn't get Mike's words out of my head. Maybe I was in denial. As much as I wanted to believe he was wrong, he really does know me better than anybody, and maybe there was some truth to what he said. Right? No. No way. He had no idea what he was talking about. What about the patience required to be married to him, or to refrain from smothering him with my pillow right there on the spot? His chest rose and fell with peaceful serenity. *What do you know about patience?* I thought, and waited for sleep to come.

Okay, let me spoil the ending: Mike was right. And little did I know, I was about to learn a hard lesson in patience.

Day one. My education began with a dull ache throbbing through my body. Everything hurt. Every inch of skin, every strand of hair.

Alarm bells started going off, and all I could think was, *Not now. Please, not now.* Work was insanely busy, and illness was a luxury I couldn't afford. I popped a couple of Tylenol and got back to work. I wasn't sick, and that was that. But whatever was percolating in my body that afternoon, it was impervious to both Tylenol and denial, and by the time I was ready to head home, I could no longer ignore it. Gripped by feverish chills and covered in a sheen of cold sweat, I gave in that day and went to bed. *Everything will be fine in the morning,* I thought.

Wrong again.

Days two, three, and four were a complete blur. The flu had violently invaded my body, and I had no choice but to wave the white flag and surrender. The only thing that gave me comfort was the thought that surely this misery would be over soon. An entire box of Kleenex, two boxes of NeoCitran, and what felt like hundreds of Tylenols later, I awoke on the fifth day feeling a little better. Most people would have taken this day to just rest and relax, maybe watch a movie or read a book, happy just to be awake and upright. Not me. I got up, showered, and went for brunch with Mike. I even posted an Instagram photo mocking whatever illness I'd just been through. See this, Flu? I'm having a great time and there's nothing you can do about it. If you don't like it, you can unfollow me.

Clearly my actions offended the universe in some way because by day six I was back on the couch, shivering and delirious once again.

Days seven and eight: terrible.

Day nine: I actually started to feel a lot better. Was that a light I saw at the end of the tunnel or a hallucination caused by delirium? I still had the nagging cough, but I felt like I was on the mend. Salvation was on its way.

Over the next few days, I told everyone I was feeling much better. I said it and said it until I started to believe it myself. Until I even started to feel it. The power of positivity, am I right?

Day thirteen was actually all right, all things considered.

But when I woke up on day fourteen with the same old fever, chills, and congestion, I was furious with myself. *How could I let this happen? When the hell is this going to be over?* I'd had enough. Again, where most people might take this as a sign and rest, I still hadn't learned my lesson. By day sixteen things were out of hand. I was deathly ill again, worse than ever, but for some reason decided to try going to work again. I barely made it through the day, and on my way home that night I finally decided it was time to see the doctor. The diagnosis: walking pneumonia. I was prescribed antibiotics and complete bed rest.

It was a serious and scary matter, but all I felt was fury. I just didn't have time for this, and I sure as hell wasn't taking any more days off. My intolerance was at an all-time high. This was over. That's it. The illness would work around my schedule, not the other way around. Leaving the doctor's that evening, I decided not to tell Mike the diagnosis. I actually convinced myself that if I took my medication and rested that night, I would feel better in the morning. Whatever miracle I was expecting didn't come.

I went to work the next day, but not for long. My poor body was predictably shutting down, and there was absolutely nothing I could do to stop it. Maybe the doctor was onto something. I finally gave in and left early. I felt defeated.

Days eighteen through twenty-one were perhaps the worst of all because on top of being sick, my boredom and frustration were becoming almost unbearable. I had missed so much work and cancelled so many plans. I was tired of being sick, and sick of being tired. This wasn't me. Once again, I decided to defy nature and go back to work, but this time Mike insisted I visit the doctor first. So I did. She took one look at me and demanded I get back to bed right away. Her demeanor implied that she would drag me there herself if I didn't go willingly.

"I can't," I whimpered. A tear started rolling down my cheek.

"Heidi, if you don't let your body rest, you're going to end up in the hospital. You have to be patient and let yourself heal."

When is this ever going to end? I thought. Would it ever? I could feel myself getting angry again. She wrote me a stronger prescription and told me to go home. Not work. Home. I agreed, but only for a minute.

Later that morning, sitting at my desk at work, I couldn't stop thinking about what my doctor had said: "You have to be patient and let yourself heal." One word in particular leapt out at me. *Patient.*

I'd been very patient, I thought. It had been weeks of torment with no end in sight. How much more patient did I have to be? Then I remembered what Mike had said during our dinner party weeks before. He'd accused me of the exact same thing. I thought I knew what patience was, but clearly, I had to be missing something. So in my delirious state I actually looked up the definition of patience: the capacity to accept or tolerate delays, problems, or suffering without becoming annoyed or anxious.

Oh my God.

As I said earlier, Mike was right. As a person in general, I wasn't patient at all, and I definitely hadn't been patient these last twenty-one days. I think you can call it an aha moment. This was a revelation that shook me to my core. All this time, patience was one of the attributes I had defined myself by, failing to notice that in my life, I had been anything but patient. My hard lesson was really starting to sink in.

I left work that day and told them I would be off for the rest of the week—or for however long it would take. There's some things you just can't rush. Around this time, I stopped counting how many days I was ill and just let myself heal. Patiently. And before I knew it, I started to feel better. I was back to my old self, but better than before: calmer and more content. This is something that will stay with me forever. I learned what patience truly means, and I couldn't wait to tell you all about it.

Questions: My War with Patience

Could you see yourself in the story? Do you have a hard time with patience?

Has patience ever been a detriment to your life?

When are you the most impatient?

Would you like to be more patient?

How could you be more patient?

"I can't change the direction of the wind, but I can adjust my sails to always reach my destination."
~ Jimmy Dean

Set the Odometer

My younger sister and I haven't always been close, but over the last few years things have really improved. Though we live in two different cities, an hour and a half apart, we're closer than we've ever been. We don't see each other often, but we call or text regularly. Sometimes both.

I love reminiscing about our childhood and chatting about our everyday lives. It feels great to be as connected as we are. Recently our talks have revolved around some health issues my sister's been going through. She's physically struggling with illness, and emotionally struggling with the question of when things are going to get better.

We've all had times like these. I've had many throughout my lifetime: times where I couldn't see the light at the end of the tunnel, just darkness I had to feel my way through. I could sympathize. Desperately wanting to give her some hope that eventually her troubles would be over, I shared a story with her.

Last summer, Mike and I decided to go for an adventure on his motorcycle. We rode up to Ottawa to reconnect with some old friends over a long weekend. The ride was amazing, and so was the rest of the weekend.

Sadly, the fun came to an end when it was time to head home. Mike checked the weather and broke the bad news to me: it was supposed to rain for the entire day. I was a little nervous, but we agreed there was no way that was going to stop us. We donned our rain gear, hopped on the Harley, and started the journey home.

We didn't feel a drop of rain for the first thirty minutes but could see dark storm clouds brewing in the distance. "How you doing back there?" Mike asked, his voice coming through the speaker in my helmet.

"I'm good, but those clouds look scary," I responded.

"We're heading into some bad weather, but hopefully it won't be for too long."

Within ten minutes, we hit the rain. Actually, the rain hit us. Not a drizzle, not a playful shower, but a fierce, torrential downpour. As the rain fell, so did the temperature. I tightened my arms around Mike.

"We're only about twenty minutes to the first rest stop," he yelled. "Are you okay back there?"

"I'm okay," I said, beginning to feel a little unsure.

The rain beat down on my helmet and bike suit, the sound of it roaring all around me. I couldn't believe how loud it was, giving the motorcycle's engine a run for its money.

When we arrived at the first rest stop, we grabbed a coffee and sat by the window. I stared out at the parking lot and watched Mike's motorcycle get assaulted by the rain. I held my coffee with both hands and savoured its warmth on my skin.

"I've looked at the weather and it doesn't look like the rain is going to let up. Are you good to keep going?" Mike asked, looking up from his phone.

"How far is it to the next stop?"

"It's only eighty-six kilometres and under an hour." He looked out at his bike and then back at me. "We can do it!" he started chanting.

I smiled at him. Of course we could do it.

"Let's do it!"

Minutes into the next leg of our journey, my confidence started to waver. I felt incredibly cold and knew I had many hours of this misery before we got home. I just wanted to be home. Warm, dry, and safe. That's when a little voice in my head, my inner Heidi, said, *You can do this! All you have to do is focus on getting to the next rest stop. Don't think about how far home is. Only concentrate on the next eighty-six kilometres.*

So for the next eighty-six kilometers, I clung to this thought as tightly as I clung to Mike. The distance home didn't seem quite so scary anymore. I couldn't believe it. I'd given myself a pep talk, and it actually seemed to be working. A very short time later, we were sitting in the next pit stop. My rain gear was wet, and I couldn't seem to get warm, but I felt quite proud of myself. Twenty minutes later we were back on the bike. Before we took off I asked Mike how far it was to the next service station.

Mike set the odometer. "We only have eighty-seven kilometres to go."

Eighty-seven? That was nothing.

"I can do this," I muttered to myself.

By the time we took our next break, my clothes were soaked through, my teeth were chattering, and the rain had felt like a barrage of small rocks pummelling my skin. But sitting there with Mike, I felt resolute in my new outlook, almost eager to confront the storm again. Almost, but not quite.

When we pulled out again I screamed out loud to myself, "It's only seventy-five kilometers this time, Heidi! You got this!"

Somehow the rain had gotten even heavier, and the wind felt like an arctic gale dead set on blowing us off the highway. But I couldn't let my mind focus on that. I needed a distraction. I decided to start talking to Mike about everything and anything. We chatted about friends, movies, and our kids. I knew I had to keep talking. His voice was very comforting inside my helmet. By the time we arrived at the next rest stop, I was shivering so uncontrollably I could hardly sip my coffee without spilling it.

"Are you okay to keep going?" Mike asked

"I'm fine," I said. My teeth chattered as I spoke.

Mike grabbed my frozen hand and gave it a reassuring squeeze. "It's only seventy kilometers to the next stop. We're almost home, Heidi."

"How far is it to the house?"

"It's about one hundred and twenty kilometres," he answered.

I sat for a minute and stared into my coffee cup, watching as the steam floated up and disappeared. I took a deep breath, looked up, and said, "Let's not stop. I can do it!"

As I climbed back on the bike, I knew the next hour and a half was going to be torture. I was soaked, freezing, and exhausted from shivering. But I knew it was mind over matter, and I wasn't giving up. The storm would break before I did.

Ten minutes down the highway Mike asked me how I was doing. I hadn't spoken a word since the last stop, and my jaw was trembling so much I could hardly answer him. "Good" was all I could get out. As we approached the next stop, Mike asked me if I wanted to take one last break. I desperately needed to get warm, but I knew I had to keep going. I answered him with an emphatic NO. As we drove past the service station, I felt an amazing euphoria wash over me. I knew the ride was almost over now. My heart started racing. I felt invigorated!

The next forty minutes flew by, and before I knew it we pulled into the driveway. Home at last. It was over. I did it!

So I told my sister, no matter what circumstance you're dealing with, whether it's a health issue or any other situation life throws at you, you just have to handle it bit by bit. When you take your problems and break them up into bite-sized little chunks, it's amazing how things that were once so daunting can suddenly seem so manageable. Just live one hurdle at a time, one chapter at a time, one day at a time. No matter what journey you're on, set your odometer and only focus on getting to the next rest stop. One day you'll arrive at your destination. Whatever you do, keep riding.

Questions: Set the Odometer

Do you get overwhelmed by your circumstances? Do things just feel so daunting?

What are you dealing with that feels never-ending?

Do you feel it would be easier if you broke it down into little chunks?

How could you break it down? By time, by goals, by actions?

What is one thing you could decide today that would make your circumstances easier to tolerate?

Are you ready to set the odometer and finally reach your destination?

"Faith is taking the first step even
when you don't see the whole staircase."
~ Martin Luther King Jr.

The Five-Gallon Pot

If there is one thing I've learned in life, it is that any sort of personal self-development has taken a lot of work. I wish there was a magic pill or an easy answer, but the simple truth of the matter is—there isn't. Throughout the years, I've worked hard to understand my own thoughts and emotions, leaning into the pain of heartbreak, setbacks, and mistakes, learning how to react and respond positively. I have realized it was never about my background, my education, or my past, but a choice to build an incredible foundation of strength, love, and resilience to handle anything life has to offer. Learning this has also inspired me to share this knowledge with anyone struggling with their own journey—always as the empathic friend with a new perspective or positive suggestion to help them find their own answers. I feel it was my way of paying it forward for all those who had done the same for me.

This time, it was a co-worker who had sent me a distressing email the night before. I immediately responded that I was happy to meet the next day to discuss his issue. The moment he sat down, he blurted, "I can't continue living with this pain anymore. I honestly feel I'm never going to be happy."

194

I felt sorry for him and compassionately asked him to tell me what happened.

"It's not just one thing. It's everything. My entire life has been one painful moment after another and I just can't take it anymore," he answered.

Realizing this wasn't going to be a quick coffee break, I settled in to give him my full attention. His story was devastating, filled with painful childhood memories, family drama, difficult decisions, mistakes, and too many setbacks to keep track of. From what I could understand, it seemed like he'd never dealt with his pain before. Each story held a raw and agonizing emotion as if it had just happened to him.

My immediate suggestion was to recommend he try journalling. It was always an impressive tool that had worked for me. I found seeing my thoughts and emotions on paper helped me work through them and then finally let them go. He quickly shot the idea down—he'd tried journalling before and it didn't work. I didn't judge his response. Not everyone loves to journal.

Next, I suggested a few of my favourite books. As an avid self-help reader, I strongly recommended he check them out. Many had been lifesavers for me. He responded, almost a little frustrated this time, that he wasn't a great reader and wouldn't read them. It was becoming obvious that no matter how many times I zigged with a positive suggestion, he would zag with an excuse or reason why it wouldn't work.

Not wanting to give up, I asked him what he felt he should do to let go of the pain. He sadly responded that it wasn't that easy and I probably just didn't understand.

He was right. I couldn't relate to what he'd been through. Yet what I did understand was he was pleading the victim and it had only resulted in a self-inflicted emotional prison sentence

195

without parole. I'd served that sentence a few times myself in the past and knew it quite well. Understanding this, I felt like I needed a completely different approach.

I began by explaining that when I moved to my Toronto home, there wasn't one tree to be found in my backyard. In fact, the only thing that existed was a deck off the back of the house and some grass. There wasn't a flower, a bush, or as I said, even a tree. As an enthusiastic gardener, the thought of a clean slate was pretty exciting. It was an incredible opportunity to create my very own backyard oasis from scratch.

My first creative decision was to buy a tree for the middle of my yard. A beautiful focal point that would eventually give some much-needed shade and become a safe haven for all the neighbourhood birds. The chosen tree was a beautiful honey locust. She was about five feet tall and lived in a five-gallon pot. When I got her home, I couldn't wait to plant her in the yard. Once I did, I stood back and admired her. She looked so small and frail compared with the rest of the yard. However, I knew it wouldn't be long before she dominated the garden.

Over the next few years, my little honey locust tree started to grow. It didn't seem like much in the beginning, but I knew her roots were quietly spreading underground, becoming her strength and support system to help her grow into the mighty tree she would become. By the fifth year, the tree no longer looked like a weak twig planted in the grass. Her trunk had quadrupled in size, and her impressive branches stretched far and wide. She was starting to look impressive.

Now eleven years later, the almighty honey locust tree is a true force of beauty and strength in our yard. She's withstood extreme summers and winters and endured torrential rain, hail, and wind storms, never uprooting herself and always adapting to every condition.

I addressed my friend: "You see, I'm sharing this story with you because you are no different from my honey locust tree. Right now, you are living your life like a little tree in a five-gallon pot. Left in the small pot, my tree would have survived just like you are surviving. However, she never would have grown past five feet. Her only opportunity to grow came once she was planted. Yet I feel this must have been daunting to her in such a large yard. You are no different, my friend.

"Learning how to deal with your pain is going to be uncomfortable and a lot of work. I also bet the thought of changing probably feels overwhelming to you. However, I need you to remember my tree didn't shrivel up and die when I planted her. On the contrary, she spread her roots and a foundation was created to grow and flourish. You can do the same.

"By opening your mind to new possibilities and opportunities, you will learn and develop new tools to finally let go of your sorrow and thrive. It is then, and only then, that you will be able to grow into the beautiful human being you are meant to be, not unlike my magnificent honey locust tree. So it is up to you. Stay inside your five-gallon pot and always be the victim, or choose to step outside your vessel and live a victorious life."

As I finished my story I noticed a tear roll down his face. He also stopped making excuses. The only words he finally spoke were, "I'm ready to be victorious!"

In the weeks that followed, I actually did notice a difference in him, a happier difference. It seemed clear he was finally starting to let go and choose a better life for himself. As for me, I was forever grateful to see another amazing tree had been planted.

Questions: The Five-Gallon Pot

Can you relate to the story? Does life feel too painful some days?

Are you making excuses and playing the victim? What excuses are you making? Be honest with yourself.

What is one thing you could do to step outside your five-gallon pot?

Are you ready to be victorious?

"Kindness is the language the deaf can hear
and the blind can see."
~ Mark Twain

Together We Can Make a Difference

In this fast-paced world, sometimes kindness can take a back seat to social media, self-interest, and our busy lives. Yet as our richest human currency, it's something we need to share for our fundamental existence. A friendly compliment, going out of your way for someone, or even giving a smile to a passerby on the street can easily make a monumental difference. Yet most of the time we don't realize or care just how necessary and life changing an act of kindness can be. At least this was the case for me during my younger years.

It was a few days before Christmas, and a girlfriend called me to see if I wanted to grab a coffee. As a new mom, I was always looking for an excuse to get out of the house. So I agreed immediately. I must have desperately needed some adult time, because two coffees later, I had barely let my friend get a word in edgewise. A mother of two herself, she completely understood and gladly let me chatter on. About halfway through another story, I noticed my friend wasn't listening anymore. She was clearly distracted by something over my shoulder. Turning around, I noticed a frantic woman trying to get her debit card to work.

"Do you know her?" I asked my friend.

"I do. Give me a minute—I'm going to go and see if I can help," she replied, standing to walk over to her.

A few minutes later, my friend returned to the table with the frantic woman in tow. Immediately I could tell she was upset. Her eyes were swollen, like she'd been crying all night. She looked pale and tired, and her hair and clothes resembled a college student who'd just rolled out of bed. After I was introduced, my friend asked her if she was okay. She admitted she wasn't and sadly burst into tears. Alarmed by her sudden outburst, I quickly jumped up to grab her some napkins as my friend consoled her.

When I returned to the table, I could sense she was a little embarrassed by her emotional response. Wanting to put her at ease, I quickly told her not to worry: I was a new mom with raging hormones and I'd already cried fourteen times that day. She laughed at my silly confession, but soon her tears were flowing again.

For the next forty-five minutes, my friend and I both sat and patiently listened to her. She revealed her humiliation after her husband had left her a few weeks earlier for another woman and her devastation when she discovered, days before Christmas, he'd heartlessly cleared out their bank accounts and left her with nothing.

Through my friend's questioning, I was able to gather that she was a stay-at-home mom of two, didn't have any siblings, and wasn't close with her family. I empathized with her situation, but I also found it incredibly difficult to believe things like this happened beyond a sensational movie plotline. In one split second, her entire life had come crashing down around her, leaving her heartbroken, alone, and destitute without an already written happy ending.

We both tried our best to cheer her up. My friend even tried to give her some cash. Yet her pride, pain, and heartache seemed stronger and fully resistant to our words of encouragement. When she finally got up to leave, she wiped her tears, thanked us both for listening, and walked out.

"Wow, can you believe her sad story?" my friend asked, shaking her head in disbelief.

"No, I can't," I answered, a little shaken by the entire encounter.

As I drove home, I couldn't stop thinking about how depressed she looked when she left the coffee shop. *No one deserves to feel that sad*, I thought, especially right before Christmas. *There must be something I can do to help.* I racked my brain for an answer.

Gladly, a solution came. I decided to help make Christmas a little special for them by buying each of them a few gifts. I knew it wouldn't solve her problems, but it could distract her from her pain for at least a day. As soon as I got home, I called my girlfriend and excitedly explained my plan. She agreed with me that it would probably be best if she delivered the presents and I remained anonymous. The woman felt humiliated enough, and the last thing I wanted to do was embarrass her anymore.

Christmas Eve morning, I drove to my friend's house and dropped off a large hamper of food and a few presents for the three of them, all addressed from Santa Claus. I honestly felt like a true Christmas Elf and loved the feeling of being able to spread some Christmas cheer.

Once my girlfriend had delivered everything, she called to report the kids were overjoyed and excited to receive their presents. However, their mom had experienced a different reaction. She seemed guilty and embarrassed to receive charity from a stranger and felt she couldn't accept the packages. Yet my friend's quick thinking diverted her attention by insisting Santa didn't accept returns. Eventually, she graciously accepted the kindness and thanked my friend. I was grateful to think the gifts may have put a smile on her face, even if it may have only been for a few short hours.

Months later, I was still thinking about her, and I asked my girlfriend if she had heard from her. Sadly, they'd lost touch, and she didn't know how to reach her. A year and a half later, as fate would have it, I saw her at the gym. I actually hardly recognized her. She looked so different. The once pale, sad, disheveled woman now looked bright, confident, and happy. My heart filled with joy to see she seemed to be doing better. I was also grateful when she walked up to me and asked if we knew each other. I reminded her I had met her with my friend over a year ago. Realizing who I was, and that I had witnessed a difficult moment in her life, she apologized for her behaviour and admitted she was doing much better. I quickly told her there was nothing to be sorry for and agreed she looked amazing.

"Thank you," she politely responded, but then seemed to be lost in thought.

"Are you okay?" I asked.

"Yes, I'm fine. You just reminded me of a significant moment," she answered.

"I'm sorry, I didn't mean to jog your mind of old wounds," I reacted, feeling a little guilty that seeing me may have brought back a painful time.

She waved off my apology. She wasn't thinking about her upsetting breakup, she reassured me. Then out of nowhere she asked if I'd ever experienced one moment that completely changed the trajectory of my life.

"I don't know—I guess. Why?" I asked, a little perplexed by her question.

She explained that after she'd left the coffee shop that day, she'd sadly decided that once Christmas was over, she was going to take her own life. She really felt it was her only option. Beyond surprised, I compassionately shared how sorry I was to hear things seemed that bad and asked her what changed her mind.

"Santa Claus happened," she answered.

Suddenly, I could feel myself blushing. *Does she know I'm the person who sent her the package?* I thought. Yet she didn't. She just wanted to share her story. In detail, she told me about my friend dropping off the gifts I had wrapped as well as her shock and gratitude that a complete stranger would go out of their way to do something so kind for her family. Apparently, it had been the kindest thing anyone had ever done for her. The gesture had actually gifted her a sense of hope when everything had seemed so hopeless.

Listening to her describe her awe-inspiring interpretation brought me to tears. I may sound naive, but I'd never realized my gesture could ever have been so powerful. I just couldn't believe a simple act of kindness had the ability to change or, even bigger than that, save someone's life. I apologized to her for my emotional reaction and then thanked her for sharing her story, never revealing it had been me who sent her the gifts. Her story was much more magical if she believed it was Santa Claus.

From that day forward, I never underestimated the power of kindness and never missed an opportunity to spread some around. A compliment to a friend or co-worker embraces so much more meaning to me now. Holding the door or even smiling at a stranger on the street is acknowledgment that I see them.

Going out of my way for someone helps me connect with people on a deeper level.

I may not be changing the entire world with these actions, but when done from the heart they can easily change someone's world entirely. So I implore all of you, spread kindness whenever possible. Big or small, any act or gesture just might change someone's day or even better than that . . . save someone's life.

Together, we can make a difference.

Questions: Together We Can Make a Difference

Can you remember an act of kindness that changed your life? What happened, and how did it change your life?

How did it make you feel?

Have you ever performed an act of kindness that changed someone's life? What did you do?

Were you surprised how much it affected the other person's life?

Were you surprised how much it affected your life?

Are you ready to make a bigger difference in the world?

Join the Positive People Army, and let's make a difference together!
www.positivepeoplearmy.com

About Heidi Allen

Heidi Allen is the Founder and President of the Positive People Army. What began as a blog has rapidly become a global movement with thousands of people from all over the world who are working together to make a difference. With previous careers as a wedding gown store owner, lifestyle editor for a popular wedding magazine,  co-host for a morning radio show, and host for six seasons of the popular wedding show, *Rich Bride, Poor Bride*, Heidi ended up as a producer on the number one daytime Canadian TV show.

The three-time award winning producer Heidi decided to leave it all to start a company whose focus was to make a real difference in people's lives. Since leaving her high-profile career, Heidi has built a positive global movement and is a sought-after motivational speaker. She lives in Toronto with her husband, Mike, and her two sons.

Heidi is living proof that when you believe in yourself and other people . . . dreams really do come true.

@positivepeoplearmy